Praise for
ACTIVE BABY, HEALTH

"Sassé's focus is on fun, but she also provides parents with an informative manual that outlines the crucial connections between movement and the health and development of body and brain." —PUBLISHERS WEEKLY

•

"A fabulous legacy for our children and an excellent contribution to the area of children's health and well-being." —OH BABY! MAGAZINE

•

"Charmingly illustrated and easy to read, this delightful book will be a boon to busy parents looking for fun ways to support their child's development."
—LINDA ACREDOLO, PHD, co-author of *Baby Minds: Brain-Building Games Your Baby Will Love*

•

"*Active Baby, Healthy Brain* provides a wealth of very informative and user-friendly information about young children's physical development. It fills a void for daily parenting skills and makes a great gift for every new parent!"
—RHONDA CLEMENTS, EDD, former President of the American Association for the Child's Right to Play, Professor of Physical Education at Manhattanville College, and author of nine books on children's games and play activities

•

"Rarely have I been presented with a book so user-friendly, complete, and profound in its breadth of understanding of early childhood development as *Active Baby, Healthy Brain*. It is truly a must-have for all new parents, grandparents, and people working with preschool children. Margaret Sassé has come to the heart of what is most essential for our precious children today—rich sensory experiences, movement, play, and human connection. She has given the world a wonderful gift."
—CARLA HANNAFORD, PHD, biologist, educator, and author of *Smart Moves: Why Learning Is Not All in Your Head* and other movement-based learning titles

THE EXPERIMENT

BECAUSE EVERY BOOK IS A TEST OF NEW IDEAS

Also by Margaret Sassé:

If Only We'd Known
Tomorrow's Children

ACTIVE BABY, HEALTHY BRAIN

*135 Fun Exercises and Activities to Maximize
Your Child's Brain Development from Birth Through Age 5 1/2*

Margaret Sassé

Illustrations by Georges McKail

Foreword by
Frances Page Glascoe, PhD
Professor of Pediatrics
Vanderbilt University

THE EXPERIMENT

NEW YORK

This book is dedicated to
Dr Mary Louise Sheil MBBS, DCH, 1934–2000 and Jean Rigby,
BA, Dip Ed, (d. 1996), for thirty years director of a New Start for the Underachiever
(ANSUA; now called Learning Connections). The work of these and other wonderful
parents was fundamental to the development of Toddler Kindy GymbaROO
in the 1970s and 1980s.

ACTIVE BABY, HEALTHY BRAIN: *135 Fun Exercises and Activities to*
Maximize Your Child's Brain Development from Birth Through Age 5½
Text copyright © Toddler Kindy GymbaROO Pty Limited, 2009, 2010
Illustrations copyright © Georges McKail 2009, 2010
Foreword copyright © Frances Page Glascoe 2009, 2010

The Experiment, LLC
260 Fifth Avenue
New York, NY 10001-6425
www.theexperimentpublishing.com

First North American edition published by arrangement with Exisle Publishing Limited.

Neither the author nor the publisher is engaged in rendering professional advice or services to individual readers and their children or relatives. The ideas, procedures, and suggestions in this book are not intended as a substitute for consulting a physician. All matters regarding health require medical supervision. Neither the author nor the publisher shall be liable or responsible for any loss, injury, or damage allegedly arising from any information or suggestion in this book. The opinions expressed in this book represent the personal views of the author and not of the publisher.

Library of Congress Control Number: 2009937033
ISBN: 978-1-61519-006-5

Cover design by Alison Forner
Cover photograph by © Blend Images/Super Stock
Text design by Christabella Designs

Manufactured in the United States of America
First printing January 2010
10 9 8 7 6 5 4 3 2

CONTENTS

Foreword by Frances Page Glascoe, PhD   9
Terms used in this book   10
Preface   13
Nutrition   14

Stage A: Birth to 6 months   15
Basic activities   15
Helping your infant's development   16
Inhibition of the primitive reflexes   17
Massage, massage, massage . . .   18
. . . and more massage   19
General infant activities   20
Infant exercises   21
Vestibular stimulation   22
Floor playtime   23
Tummy time is vital   24
Brain stimulation: dancing   25
Music for all ages   26
Exercises: 2–6 months   27
Exercises for hips and limbs   28
Vestibular fun   29
More vestibular fun   30
Nursery rhymes, rhythm, and song   31
Vision: Birth to 2 months   32
Vision: 2–6 months   33
Forward movement: 3–6 months   34
Muscle tone development   35
Legs, feet, and hands stimulation   36
Movement stimulation   37
Vestibular stimulation   38

Stage B: 6–12 months   39
Creeping, cruising, walking   39
Massage   40
Massage, exercises, music   41
Tummy time   42
Crawling on the front   43

Bottom shufflers   44
Shoulders, arms, and hands development   45
Balance through muscle tone stimulation   46
Creeping activities   47
Ladders   48
Cruising, bobbing, and thinking   49
Exercises: 10–12 months   50
Dancing   51
Rocking, swinging, and jiggling   52
Visualization   53

Stage C: Walking to 18 months   54
Massage, music, and songs   55
Basic motor planning: 12–15 months   56
Balance: 15–18 months   57
Developmental activities: 15–18 months   58
Upper body development: 15–18 months   59
Vestibular stimulation   60
Rolling and tipping backward   61
Rockin' and rollin'   62
Music, rhythm, and song   63
Dance exercises   64
Vision   65
Visualization   66

Stage D: 18–24 months   67
Massage   68
Massage through exercise and song   69
Exercise to music   70
Nursery rhyme movements   71
Muscle tone development   72
Upper body development   73
Animal locomotion   74
Vestibular bending and spinning   75
Wheelbarrows, swinging, and spinning   76
Balance   77
Further Balance   78
Rhythm band   79
Motor planning through dance   80
Sensory motor perceptual activities   81
Beanbags and balloons   82
Balls   83

Hoops   84
Ribbons and cords   85
Visual tracking   86
Visualization   87

Stage E: 2–2½ years   88
Massage in crocodile position   89
Angels in the sand   90
Body awareness and vestibular stimulation   91
Rolling and tumbling   92
Swinging and spinning   93
Wobble board and balance beam   94
Motor planning: dance   95
Music, rhythm, nursery rhymes, and songs   96
Rhythm sticks   97
Beanbags   98
Balls   99
Hoops   100
Ribbons and cords   101
Vision   102
Visualization   103

Stage F: 2½–3½ years   104
Massage in crocodile position   105
Tiger creeping   106
Finger awareness   107
Mini-trampoline exercises   108
Body awareness and concepts   109
Spinning and swinging   110
Animal balance positions   111
Wobble board   112
Laterality for 3-year-olds   113
Cross-pattern movements   114
Music, dance, and rhythm   115
Rhythm sticks   116
Beanbags   117
Balls   118
Hoops   119
Ribbons and cords   120
Visual stimulation   121
Visualization   122

Stage G: 3½–4½ years   123

Massage and cross-pattern commando   124
Angels in the sand   125
Balance   126
Scooter boards   127
Mini-trampoline   128
Laterality   129
Dance   130
Rhythm sticks for 3-year-olds   131
Rhythm sticks for 4-year-olds   132
Beanbags   133
Balls   134
Hoops   135
Ropes and cords   136
Vision   137
Visualization   138

Stage H: 4½–5½ years   139

Massage: crocodile and commando positions 140
Squirming, crawling, and creeping   141
Tumbling, rocking, swinging   142
Balance   143
Mini-trampoline   144
Cross-pattern actions   145
Aerobic dance   146
Rest period with Mozart   147
Homemade band   148
Rhythm sticks   149
Beanbags   150
Balls   151
Hoops   152
Ropes and cords   153
Vision   154
Visualization   155

Bibliography   156
Index   159

FOREWORD

Margaret Sassé, the creator of GymbaROO, was a leading international authority on the value (and enormous fun) of movement in children's lives—and in parents' lives, too. I visited GymbaROO's infant and toddler classes in 2008 and it was a joyous experience. Children were engaged, excited, moving in novel ways—and they were learning critical pre-literacy and language skills.

Particularly interesting was the fact that the accompanying parents were mostly fathers. Dads don't always know how to engage their very young children. Meanwhile, research consistently demonstrates that fathers' involvement in children's lives is associated with subsequent school success.

Today's children definitely don't move around enough. Obesity is the common consequence and it is extremely hazardous to health, well-being and learning. Movement, play, and active exploration are essential to children's development. So, parents, have fun with this book. You will enjoy the many suggestions for worthwhile ways to engage your child, whether he/she is an infant or preschooler. Both you and your child will not only learn lots but also learn together—with mirth and happiness.

Frances Page Glascoe, PhD
Professor of Pediatrics
Vanderbilt University
Nashville, Tennessee

TERMS USED IN THIS BOOK

Concept development: Educationally, "concept" refers to such terms as above / below, in front / behind, up / down, wide / narrow. There are seventy-eight such concepts relating to the body, movement, effort, speed, direction, and space awareness.

Cross-pattern movement: The standard walking movement, where the right arm and left foot go forward, then the left arm and right foot. It's also the norm in running, throwing, and other similar activities.

Directionality: Directionality is often confused with *laterality*. It is an awareness of space *outside* the body.

Fine motor skills: Usually dependent on gross motor skills, these refer to the use of the small muscles of the body required for handling utensils such as pencils and fine instruments. Eye movements are dependent on the fine muscles of the visual tract.

Gross motor skills: Large body movement such as jumping, hopping, walking, and climbing.

Inhibition: Refers to the overcoming but not removal of specific *primitive reflexes*. Accident or illness may cause the brain to allow these reflexes to resurface to assist survival. Remnants of primitive reflexes can cause "hiccups" (difficulties) in development and learning.

Laterality: In child development, this refers to the ability to use each side of the body independently or together when doing a task; for example, when using scissors correctly, one hand cuts with the scissors and the other holds the object to be cut. Laterality is the motor basis for spatial concepts. *Bilaterality* refers to two sides working together, often doing the same thing, such as an infant riding a scooter, pushing with both feet together.

Primitive reflexes: These are the unconscious movements that occur both before and after birth. They cause such survival skills as sucking, before the connections to the higher brain have been established, and provide rudimentary training for later voluntary skills. Primitive reflexes are taken over by voluntary movements, provided there are favorable environmental factors to create sufficient stimulation.

Postural reflexes: These reflexes follow after the primitive reflexes and stay for life, such as the parachute reflex, when our arms fly forward if we go upside down, or the balance reflex, when we automatically regain our balance by using one side of our body against the other to stop ourselves from falling.

Sensory integration: This occurs when the brain puts together and uses all the information received from the ears, eyes, skin, nose, tongue, muscles, and joints as a basis for ongoing development.

Sensory motor perceptual activities: The coming together of sensory stimulation (hearing, seeing, feeling, tasting, and internal body messages from the muscles and ligaments) to make sense or create understanding, which is called *perception*.

Sequential pathways: Sequential means one after the other, indicating a successive series of movements for coordination or auditory requests or rote learning, which stimulate specific "pathways" or neural tracts in the brain.

Temporal awareness: Rate, time, and sequence of movements, actions, or rhythm.

Vestibular stimulation: Stimulation of the fluid in the inner ear over the thousands of tiny hairlike cells surrounding its surface. These cells are vital to knowledge of our position in space, and play a big role in *sensory integration*.

Visualization: The ability of the brain to "see in the mind's eye," and thus remember a pattern of movement, a sequence of sounds, or the look and feel of things, including word and letter formations.

Visual tracking: Following a moving target with either one eye or both— *without* moving the head.

Note: The text of this book has been written to give equal weight to each gender, so the example of a boy is used in Stages A, C, E, and G, while a girl is used in Stages B, D, F, and H. Illustrations are mixed. All exercises are intended for all children regardless of gender.

SPIRAL OF DEVELOPMENT

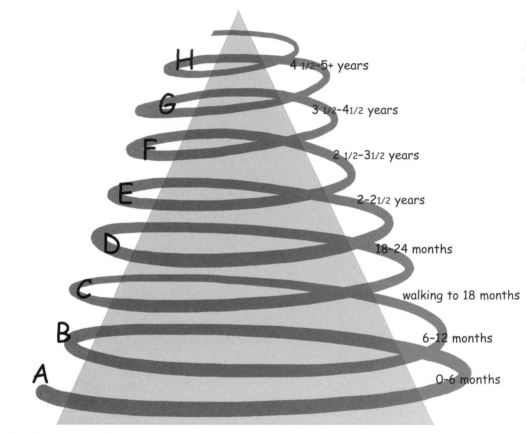

H   4 1/2–5+ years

G   3 1/2–41/2 years

F   2 1/2–31/2 years

E   2–21/2 years

D   18–24 months

C   walking to 18 months

B   6–12 months

A   0–6 months

developmental stage   age-group

PREFACE

The main aim of this book is to help parents maximize the critical periods of brain development during the first years of life. Brain development continues throughout life, depending on the environmental stimuli.

Nature has provided a natural, predictable, sequential development for everyone, from conception. The initial movements are called *reflexes*, which stimulate the growth of pathways within the brain to assist in the development of the voluntary movements and learning capacity of the individual.

The activities in the book are sequentially arranged and are important for developing the foundations needed for successful learning. Each child's rate of development differs. Ideally all children will pass through these normal, sequential, predictable stages.

You can nurture your child's development by providing opportunities for your child to enjoy and participate in the activities described in the book. Choose activities in the area of massage, inner-ear (vestibular) stimulation, and movements appropriate to age to form a small ten-minute program to be done several times daily. As the baby becomes a toddler, this is not so easy and is best done in a sequential, fun way while playing games with them or reading their favorite books. Just set aside regular ten-minute periods every day to play the *Smart Start* game.

No activity should last for more than two minutes, and it should be done *slowly*. Remember: *intensity*, *frequency*, and *duration* are the keys to development. The name of the game is *repetition*: children do this instinctively. Where there has been some minor "hiccup" causing a developmental delay, then the frequency, intensity, and duration are key factors of considerable importance.

NUTRITION

The type of food we eat can have a significant effect on the course of development. This section on nutrition covers all stages of early childhood.

Food is fuel for the brain as well as the body. It drives growth, energy, cell repair, and hormonal balance. The quality, variety, and timing of food intake can have a major effect on development, health, and learning. Energy from food is more efficient when a person is moving.

It is vital that all parents think carefully about the effects of artificial colorings, additives, and excessive sugar when considering their child's development, learning, and behavior. Many chemicals and foods can trigger and sustain behavioral and/or learning difficulties in children. The intake of foods with artificial coloring and preservatives or excessive sugar should be carefully monitored.

Adverse reactions to some common food groups are also *not* uncommon. For example, some children may be sensitive to wheat or dairy foods. Salicylates in berries and stone fruits will send some children "haywire."

While there are some who deny that chemicals in food seriously affect children, many parents attest to the fact that their children react adversely to chemicals. Parents are frequently blamed for a child's abnormal behavior, which may be grossly unfair to the child, the family, and the community. All it takes is a small amount of a chemical in food to affect some children. Like sugar, these small amounts can be added to foods—and this can be done without labelling.

Children with food and chemical sensitivities are often diagnosed as having autistic spectrum syndromes, attention-deficit hyperactivity disorder (ADHD), and so on, as their symptoms are often similar. Biting, swearing, kicking, lack of attention, sensory sensitivities, "turning off," and other behavioral problems are some of the warning signs.

In my experience, increased stimulation through movement can rarely prevent difficulties arising from an unsatisfactory diet or adverse reactions to specific foods.

Watch what your child is eating!

For further information on food additives and chemical sensitivities, check the website of the Food Intolerance Network: www.fedupwithfoodadditives.info

STAGE A: BIRTH TO 6 MONTHS

BASIC ACTIVITIES

- Breast-feeding is nature's plan, but is not always possible.
- Ask your specialist for advice on formulas.
- Feed your infant from both the right and left side if bottle feeding. This is important in order to stimulate each side of your infant's body and allow each hand to open and shut as it grabs at the mother's breast and clothing.

Lifting infant to lie on his back
Pick your infant up so his head rests in the crook of your arm, first one side and then the other. Repeat three to five times.

Lifting infant to lie on his front
Try the same with your infant lying on his front across your arm, looking downward.

Lifting infant to sitting position
Have your infant sitting on one arm, while holding his back firmly against you with your other hand.

Lay infants on their fronts (*when awake*) as soon as possible after birth— some say five days—so they become accustomed to this position, which enables the repetitive "wriggling" reflex of newborn infants. This is very important for overcoming the primitive, involuntary survival reflexes of infancy. Front lying also strengthens the infant's neck, which is vital for the overcoming of the primitive reflexes, allowing the development of voluntary movements of infancy.

HELPING YOUR INFANT'S DEVELOPMENT

- The hearing pathways are more mature at birth than the visual pathways.
- While your infant is asleep, play low-volume music or nature sounds.
- Sing and move to music—dance to the beat.
- All coordinated movements require rhythm and stimulate speech and language.
- Every day, read simple rhythmical stories and nursery rhymes with repetitive language.
- Massage and exercise your infant slowly to enable the messages to be absorbed through the central nervous system to the brain.

Infants love the soothing rhythmic movement of dance. This is both massage and inner-ear (vestibular) stimulation. The basic elements of dance are space, form, time, flow, rhythm, and emotional response. Dancing with infants helps in the development of balance and space and body awareness. Little ones under 2–3 months of age do not have adequate neck muscles to lift their own head, so support the head in all activities for this age.

Bonding
Massage, rock, and dance with your infant to develop bonding. Look directly into his eyes as you talk lovingly and sing.
Pat your infant to the beat of your song.
Be sure his cradle can be rocked.

INHIBITION OF THE PRIMITIVE REFLEXES

- Infants must learn about their body so they can move.
- Movement creates brain development and is the result of inborn primitive reflexes (unconscious movements), which develop in early pregnancy and are present at birth.
- Many reflexes are involved in a child's development.
- Voluntary control of the primitive reflexes occurs through massage of the skin and nerve endings under the skin in joints, muscles, ligaments, and in the inner ear.

Worm squirm

This primitive reflex is present before and after birth to 3–4 months of age. It is vital to future development.

All parents have seen their infant (when on his front) "squirm" forward. By the age of two, a toddler can be asked to be a worm wriggling along to improve awareness of each side of his body.

Bouncing and swaying

From four weeks of age, lay your infant on his front, holding him firmly under his chest, and encourage him to lift his head in order to strengthen his neck and shoulder muscles. This will help him gain voluntary control over the primitive reflexes, which are influenced by head movement. Bounce and sway.

MASSAGE, MASSAGE, MASSAGE . . .

- Start massage as soon as possible after birth.
- At birth your infant sees, hears, and feels, but does not understand.
- There are no set rules: follow your instincts and his reactions.
- Sing and smile while you gently stroke and squeeze him.
- He needs to be without clothing and lying on a warm towel.
- Ensure the lotion, your hands, and the room are warm.
- Be gentle, and always support the head when rolling him over.

Whole body relaxation

Put your child on a slightly inflated big beach ball.
Gentle bouncing of the ball will create full relaxation.
Move his arms in and out very slowly and
gently, then move the legs up and down.
Finally, play gentle pull-ups to create
some muscle tone.
Support his head and neck.
These actions will massage his
ligaments and muscles.

Massage body front and back

With a circular clockwise movement, massage the stomach,
then slide your hands down the sides from the waist.
With the infant on his front, stroke the whole body,
then roll him over supporting the head. With
slow circular movements, continue down his spine and back
Use a light playful pinching action over the buttocks.

The brain controls learning. Nature has provided a superb predictable, sequential series of movements to help brain development. By two months of age you can use more materials, and vary the massage, such as tapping with fingers.

... AND MORE MASSAGE

- Use a light touch and at other times deep firm strokes or squeezes.
- Start with blowing fun, by gently blowing their palms and other body parts. They love this gentle feeling all over their bodies.
- Music, humming, and singing are food for the brain and the ears. Make up a song that identifies the body parts. Rhymes provide the rhythm of music.

Light massage provides delicate touch and movement stimulation to the nerve endings. Massage stimulates an awareness of body parts.

Massage head and chest

Start with long flowing strokes from head to toes. Trace circles gently on the head. Enclose the head with both hands, and gently massage the scalp. Stroke gently down the face, stroking eyes and nose with the fingers. Stroke from the rib cage out across the shoulders, and downward.

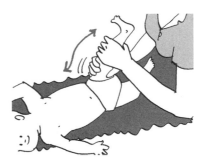

Massage the arms

Start with whole body strokes. Massage from hands to the shoulder—then hands, individual fingers, and palms.

Massage legs and feet

Use the thumb to massage over the top of the foot, then toward the ankles. Roll and squeeze each toe.

GENERAL INFANT ACTIVITIES

- While feeding your child, encourage the grasping and sucking reflex that causes the opening and closing of the hand as he sucks. If remnants of this reflex are still present at school age, handwriting problems may occur.
- If bottle-feeding, change sides from right to left as you would if breast-feeding, so that both sides of his body get movement stimulation.

Leg and tummy development at 2–3 months

Lift up the legs by lifting the infant's buttocks. The infant will flex the legs upward; lower him and the legs will straighten. This strengthens the tummy muscles for later movements.

Be gentle—these activities must not cause crying! Do not become a victim of infant tyranny. Hold your infant gently but firmly, and give support especially around the neck and head area. Poor muscle tone frequently equals poor coordination, as the body parts cannot put movements together! Rocking stimulates the organs of muscle tone and balance, as well as strengthening neck muscles for head control.

Rocking sideways

Gently rock your child on his back from side to side. He will move his head accordingly. Do not turn him more than 45 degrees.

INFANT EXERCISES

Lying on the front strengthens the infant's head, neck, and shoulder muscles, vital for overcoming primitive reflexes. If your infant has sucking difficulties, be guided by your lactation specialist. If he is put on to formula, watch for any unsettled crying or skin rashes, in case his constitution objects to the formula.

Gentle turnovers

With your infant on his back, turn him gently by bending one leg up (his arm on the same side will swing over across his chest), then gently push the leg by the bent knee over and across the body. He will lift his 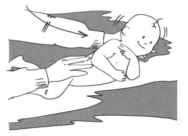 head slightly, strengthening the neck muscles. Turn him in this way, from back to front and back again *slowly*, several times. Place your right hand gently under his head for support.

Arm movements

Slowly move arms up and down together and alternately in and out, as above. This is also suitable for month-old infants.

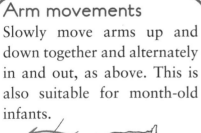

Pushaways with infant on his back

Use the palms of your hand or a rolled cloth to activate the reflex stretch of one leg and then the other. Press against the foot with a gentle force, to make him push your hand away.

These exercises aim to relax the limbs of infants and develop muscle tone and body awareness. Ensure the limbs are fully extended, but do not force. Exercises should be done slowly and gently.

VESTIBULAR STIMULATION

The inner ear contains a very complex structure and is responsible for balance and hearing, as well as gravity and movement.

Infants need you to provide opportunities to stimulate their vestibular system. Vestibular activities are essential for the inhibition of the primitive reflexes and the development of balance.
Vestibular sensations are vital for posture, movement, and a sense of position in space, motion, depth, and self.

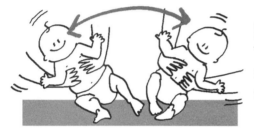

Rocking from side to side
With your baby seated, rock him from side to side. Note the grip on the infant.

Rocking back and forth
Rock your infant forward and back (for children aged 2–3 months). The aim is to allow him to hold his head up, but support it if necessary—do not allow it to flop.

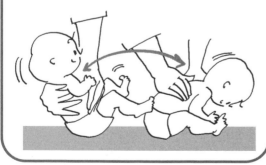

Swinging and swaying
Make a hammock swing, with one person holding each end of a blanket. Place your infant in the hammock and sway him to and fro.

FLOOR PLAYTIME

Infants who are unsettled often have eczema, skin rashes, constipation, diarrhea, repeated ear infections, tonsillitis or respiratory infections. Ask advice from your medical professionals or infant welfare specialists.

Try these activities to strengthen your infant's neck muscles, gently and just a few times right after diaper-change time, as your baby is already on her back.

Without good muscle tone in the neck area, the unconscious reflexes of nature, which stimulate initial movement and development in infants, handicap the neck in its ability to function.

Pushaways with infants from four weeks of age, on their front

Place your infant on his front with your hand against both feet with the legs bent. He will push and move away from your hand on his tummy. This is the beginning of movement forward on his front (crawling). The push works best when the legs are only slightly bent. Try this for ½–1 minute. Little and often is best.

Rolling over and back

Play with your infant on the mat. With eye-tracking, the sooner he can turn his head, the sooner visual tracking begins.

Rattles are great for encouraging head-turning. The main aim is to encourage head-lifting, to strengthen his neck muscles.

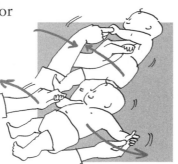

These activities promote the overcoming of the primitive survival reflexes, so that conscious movements can occur. Tummy time is important to the future development of your child. Start laying your infant on his front when he is a few weeks old, for short periods while awake, so he will learn to love this position for play.

TUMMY TIME IS VITAL

- Infants love being read to, hearing the varying pitches and the security of a kind voice, and also watching the pages of the book turn.
- Give him lots of cuddles and hugs.
- Lying on the tummy when awake will encourage drainage of the tubes between the ears and nose, which may block and cause ear infections.

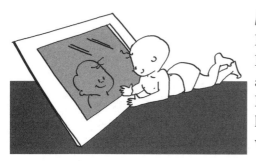

Mirror image
Prop a mirror in front of your infant. Play games with your mirror image and his.
Remember—it is hard for him to lift his head, so even a few seconds is worthwhile.

Playing propped over a roll
Provide a small roll for your infant, to free his hands for playing.
It will also help him lie on his front while playing.

Tummy time is to encourage movement so that the brain pathways are stimulated. Lying babies on their backs all the time prevents early movements and inhibits the use of both sides of the body.
Development and learning occur when the nerve endings in the muscles and ligaments of the body are stimulated.
Give your infant lots of tummy time, even if only for a minute each time.

BRAIN STIMULATION: DANCING

Dancing and music are a vital part of every day. Songs provide opportunities for rhythm, memory training, and coordination, even at this early stage. The nerve endings in the inner ear need to be stimulated, so they can send messages to the brain to help balance and to develop body and space awareness and muscle tone.

Reduce the volume on the TV or radio while you bounce, sway, spin, and sing to your infant. Dance allows for imitation, repetition, coordination, and exploration of movement to the rhythm, mood, and feeling of music. Infants were rocked and swayed in the womb for nine months and the gentle movement of dancing is a repeat of this soothing stimulation. Hold your infant gently and securely against your body, supporting the head if necessary. This way he receives visual stimulation.

Form a circle with a group of other parents and children and dance, holding your infant in front of you. The infants will be swished gently into the middle and back, with variations of jiggling, gentle stamping, running, swaying, bouncing, rocking, or even tipping the children down a little as the parents lean forward.

Be sure to protect your infant's neck at all times.

At home, walk around keeping the beat!

MUSIC FOR ALL AGES

- Newborn babies learn by hearing sounds at different levels and different tones.
- Music can be soothing or stimulating and can affect moods.
- Recognition of varying sounds is vital for speech. Words are learned by being heard constantly.

Listening is the processing of sound, along with messages received from the other senses.

Hearing is the passive reception of sound.

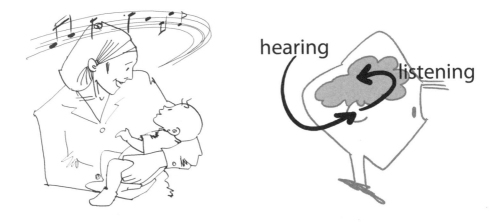

hearing
listening

Rhythm and music go together. Rhythm is part of every gesture. Movement activities with rhythm and music experiences are important, even during the first few months of life. Music and songs have different beats, tones, and levels of sound. Hearing classical music, especially by Mozart, Vivaldi, and other Baroque composers, creates a "micromassage of the muscles of the middle ear." This allows the auditory (hearing) area of the cortex (the brain) to create total brain stimulation, which can affect the rest of the nervous system, giving both physical and mental benefits. There are many specifically activated music CDs available for infants and young children.

EXERCISES: 2–6 MONTHS

- Exercises help your infant organize sensations in the brain.
- The more opportunities for practice, the more automatic your infant's responses will become.
- Rolling over at first is often accidental, as he reaches for a toy.

Lots of rolling

Encourage rolling—turning over and back at will.

Encourage him to roll down a slope, such as a mattress propped up at one end.

Rolling up and down in a blanket is fun.

Exercises for feet

Point and flex the feet and get the reflexes working.

Pressure on the heel causes extension of the toes, and pressure on the sole causes flexion of the toes.

The legs will often bend and then also straighten.

Foot reflexes are important for later walking. Touch and feeling through the skin are important for body awareness. Inhibition of the primitive reflexes is a continuing activity, as the neck and back strengthen.

Neck and back strengthening

With your infant on his back, hold both his hands and slowly but gently raise him off the floor/mattress. This exercise will strengthen the muscles of the neck, shoulders and elbows. Be prepared for "head lag" (as shown in the illustration) and *stop* once this occurs.

EXERCISES FOR HIPS AND LIMBS

• Each activity develops building blocks that will be the basis for more complex functions later.

• Forward tummy movement sends the brain more messages from muscles, ligaments, and joints and teaches the infant about his body and how it moves.

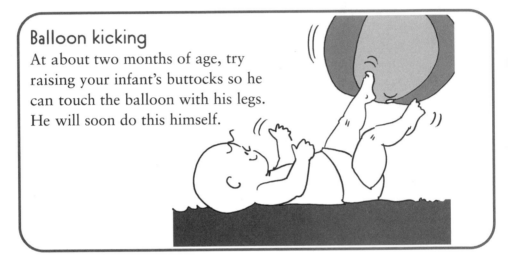

Balloon kicking

At about two months of age, try raising your infant's buttocks so he can touch the balloon with his legs. He will soon do this himself.

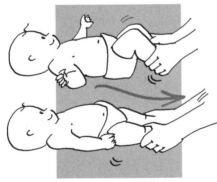

Leg exercises

Bend and straighten the infant's legs, together and individually, up and down, out and in, to the beat of a nursery rhyme. Try this exercise at every diaper change.

Lift up his bottom and say "Boo!" while the legs are apart.

Moving is your infant's workout.
Moving sends your baby's brain information about his world.
Try a little massage if there is any resistance.

VESTIBULAR FUN

Rocking on rocking chairs and swinging cradles gives gentle vestibular stimulation that helps to lull infants to sleep. Studies show that infants given regular vestibular stimulation in the first few months of life show accelerated development in motor skills, due to increased sensory stimulation.

Half rocking tip forward
Hold infant around the waist in a half-standing position, and rock him back and forth.
Sing:
Here we go rocking,
forward and backward,
Here we go rocking,
Just like this.

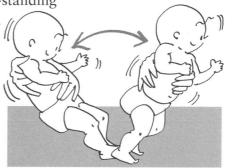

Bobbing up and down
Hold your infant firmly around the chest from behind and bob him up and down. The aim is for the knees to flex and then for the feet to push up.

Stroller rides over bumpy ground
The shoulder of a footpath, if not too bumpy, can provide comforting and stimulating rocking and swinging motions.

The inner ear is a very complex structure, which contains the hearing and vestibular nerve endings. Stimulation of the nerve endings in the inner ear creates vital sensory information, which helps unify all other sensory and motor information relayed to the brain. This stimulation is important for the development of posture, balance, coordination, movement, and vision as well as hearing.

MORE VESTIBULAR FUN

Vestibular stimulation has a positive effect on the development of speech and language, as the hearing system works closely with the vestibular system.

Clapping, tapping, chanting children's songs and nursery rhymes, rolling, tumbling, rocking, bouncing, and swinging all help the brain coordinate movement. The vestibular system functions like a traffic cop. It coordinates information from all the sensory systems and tells each sensation where to go and when it should stop.

Rolling

Rocking, rolling, or bouncing on Mom's knees or on a medium-sized ball is fun.
Sing:
[Jamie] is rocking, rolling, bouncing,
[Jamie] is rocking, rolling, or bouncing,
Just like this.

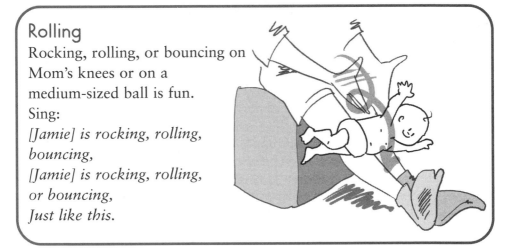

Swinging through space

Swinging infants in your arms or slow-spinning them on your lap in an office chair, is important for counteracting one of the early primitive reflexes. This is excellent vestibular stimulation. Once your infant has learned to sit independently, infant swings are an easy alternative!

NURSERY RHYMES, RHYTHM, AND SONG

Repetition is very important to infants. Every culture has its own lullabies and nursery rhymes/songs. Sing or say the rhymes repeatedly to exercises, even if the words are nonsense, as it helps speech development.

Nursery rhymes/songs
Always sing or play a well-known rhyme while doing movement activities.

Can you act out a song? For example:

Jack and Jill
Actions can be done from six weeks. Support your infant if necessary, as his muscle tone at birth may not have been strong.

Jack and Jill went up the hill to fetch a pail of water.
(Holding your infant firmly around the waist, slowly raise him a little above your head. The aim is for him to raise his head for "up the hill.")
Jack fell down and broke his crown,
(Bring him down slowly.)
And Jill came tumbling after.
(Holding him, rock him from side to side.)

Nursery rhymes provide a resource for combining movement, sensory motor stimulation, and rhythm.
Movements such as bouncing, rolling, and moving sideways and backward all stimulate rhythm, as well as balance.

VISION: BIRTH TO 2 MONTHS

- At birth your infant has sight but no vision. Light and movement equals vision. Vision is developing all the time.
- Lots of tummy time while your infant is awake is important even if only for a few minutes.

Dim light in your infant's room

To help your infant stimulate his eyes, show him flickering lights, as in Christmas tree lights, for a few minutes, four times a day.

Mobiles

Hang a mobile about 8–12 inches from the cot so that it is in line with his gaze. Move it to the other side every few days. At this age nearby objects are hard to see in clear focus.

Sight means you can see. Vision means you make sense out of what is seen. Vision is developed and learned from sensory messages the brain receives from movement, touch, hearing, smell, and taste. All activities that stimulate the inner ear also stimulate vision. The muscles controlling the eyes are affected by inner ear functions.

Near vision

From birth, be sure your infant is placed on his front when awake. This is vital for many reasons, and especially for near point vision development. Prop him with a pillow under his arms if necessary.

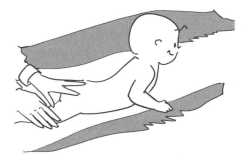

VISION: 2–6 MONTHS

Your infant's movement and sense of touch will tell him more about his world than his eyes do in the first months of life.

Bring mobiles closer at about 2–3 months, as infants need the visual experience involved in watching the object. Mobiles help develop depth perception and distance judgements. As the child waves his tight little fist, he will accidentally hit the object and eventually open his hand to grasp it.

Near point vision

At two months of age, show your infant his hands, then move them about in front of his eyes. Encourage him to follow the movement with his eyes.

Crib mobiles provide excellent visual stimulation during this period.

Rattles

Encourage your infant to turn his head to the sound of a rattle about an arm's length from his eyes. This action also requires neck control as the head is turned and visual adjustment is required.

By the end of this period, infants will be able to follow moving objects with their eyes and be able to coordinate eye and hand movements.

Vision cannot be developed alone, but does so in close relationship with other senses, so make sure that your infant not only sees but also hears, feels, and tastes the object. Your infant should not only see the rattle but also know it makes a certain sound. Help your infant to coordinate vision, hearing, and movement, as he learns and thinks in a more developed way. When an infant is touched with warmth and care, the brain is flooded with hormones that enable his brain to form more connections. Over the next few years these connections build up a network of neurons in the brain.

FORWARD MOVEMENT:
3–6 MONTHS

Now your infant is moving and squirming around on the floor, and some are even beginning to move backward. They will soon be commando crawling forward as they prepare to enter another stage up the spiral of development.

Repetitive movement on the floor, forward or backward, stimulates the neurons in the brain to interconnect. With better coordinated movement, your infant can set off to explore his world.

- This section provides stimulating activities for more active infants as they move into the period of active exploration.
- Massage at this stage is much the same as before, but becomes more difficult with moving infants. Sometimes it is easier to have your infant across your knees on his front while massaging.
- Get down on the floor with your infant and make the floor an exciting place for him to be.
- Rattles are a constant source of entertainment and stimulation, both through hearing and through watching and tracking.

- Do not sit your infant until he has enough muscle tone to support himself.
- Don't worry if your infant does not move forward in this period.
- Make sure you keep up the regular and now longer periods of tummy time when he is awake.

MUSCLE TONE DEVELOPMENT

- The development of hearing and muscle tone is now allowing your infant to make more babbling sounds. Encourage this by rhythmical singing and talking.
- Have a conversation with your infant by taking turns. He may only move his head, eyes, or mouth, or make cooing or babbling noises, but this indicates that he is listening.

Pull-ups

Pull-ups continue to strengthen neck, back, and shoulder muscles. Support the head if any head lag is noticed. With your infant lying on your legs, gently pull him up to a sitting position.

Parachute reflex

Rocking back and forth to pick up a toy promotes hand/eye coordination and stimulates the parachute reflex, which occurs when the arms go forward to prevent a fall. Hold your infant at the hips or upper thighs or in a fabric sling as he rolls forward.

Push-ups

With your infant on his tummy, grasp him firmly around the pelvis and lift.

The arms will push up and straighten as you lift them off the floor. This is a repeat exercise, but now done with more frequency and duration!

These activities strengthen the neck and back muscles and also stimulate spatial awareness and visual adjustment.
Many of the previous activities are still applicable and are easier now.
As the infant's brain develops, new skills become possible. Frequency and increased duration are now becoming the keys to all activities.

LEGS, FEET, AND HANDS STIMULATION

Inhibition of the foot reflex requires bare feet and lots of massage. Babies must be able to feel in order to move.

The feet and toes need to be flexible for balance. This is developed through movement.

Exercises for the legs stimulate muscle tone, especially knee flexibility for later bobbing, climbing, and walking.

The development of the legs and feet starts in infancy and requires stimulation through sensory inputs to the brain. It is early movement that provides so many sensory messages to the brain. "What you don't use, you lose." There are critical periods for brain cell stimulation in the first year of life.

Balloon hitting

With your infant lying on his back, hitting a hanging balloon with his hands and feet is fun. By the fifth or sixth month, some infants may bring the balloon from their feet to their hands.

Hey—these must be my feet!

Allow your infant a little time on his back to find his feet. He will love to rock back and forth as he learns to flex his knees, raise his bottom, and suck his toes. Through this activity children not only learn about their legs and feet but also how to move them at will.

MOVEMENT STIMULATION

By 5–6 months of age, some infants are refusing both breast milk and formula. If your infant is not satisfied with your feeding it may be an early sign of food sensitivity. If you have concerns, check with your maternal and child care professional.

Mat time

With head well up, tummy time on the mat now involves more movement, as infants gain voluntary control over the reflex movements.

Rolling on a pouffe or ball

With your infant lying on his tummy on the ball, roll slowly one way, then the other. This strengthens the neck, is good for head control, and provides muscle tone development.

Balance reflex development

Lay your infant on his back on a beach ball, grasp his thighs, then slowly tip the ball forward and sideways. He will slowly tense his tummy muscles as his balance reflexes develop. Also rock him on his front.

During this period, infants learn to move their limbs in coordination through space. In doing so, they gain visual, hearing, touch, smell, taste, and muscle development and head position control. Head control is necessary for forward movement, overcoming the primitive reflexes, and for developing muscle tone. Some babies are already moving on their tummies in a crocodile crawl.

VESTIBULAR STIMULATION

These activities are great for motor sensory stimulation, as the infant is whizzed slowly and carefully up, down and around.

Rocking

Rock the infant so that he is alternately lying and standing. First lie him on your outstretched legs with his feet against your stomach. Then stand him up while you rock backward. Ten times is plenty!

Whizzing from side to side

Sit your infant on your lap with his legs around your waist. Hold them tight as you whiz them from side to side.
Sing: *"Here we go whizzing around and around . . ."*
Keep eye contact!

Up, up, up, then down, down, down

Keeping the child vertically upright, lift and lower him to bobbing position. Hold him under the arms and do *not* allow him to take the weight on his feet.

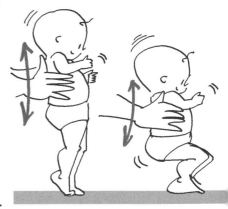

- These activities create strong sensory messages to the brain—about his position in space, how to move his eyes while changing positions, which muscles are needed to keep the body in position—and they are particularly stimulating for speech.
- Only try what you fully understand. Practice with a doll or toy animal if unsure.
- Activities should be done one to three times only.

STAGE B: 6–12 MONTHS

CREEPING, CRUISING, WALKING

Most infants are on the verge of moving or are already crocodile crawling on their stomachs, creeping (on hands and knees) and cruising. Crawling and creeping create important brain pathways. Most infants crawl, then creep for approximately five months before cruising, and finally walking, but these periods vary. Cruising is not walking; infants often do both for months.

- Once infants are mobile, danger-proof your home: cover all electrical outlets and lock away valuables.

- Keep floors clean, but allow freedom for your infant to investigate her world. Playpens restrict movement, so put yourself and the ironing in the playpen instead.

- Use safety gates and leave the pots and pans cupboard accessible (see page 43). These are vital times for sensory motor stimulation and brain growth.

- Never put your child in a walker—she needs to crawl and creep for natural development. Infant walkers can be dangerous.

- Cruising around furniture frequently occurs at the same time as creeping, as the same reflex is involved.

MASSAGE

Our skin receives signals from the environment, which are transferred to nerve centers for relaying to the brain for deciphering and, if necessary, motor action. Therefore when we feel cold, we put on more clothing if possible! Massage for this age group becomes a case of "catch me if you can."

Bath time

- In the bath or while drying your infant, use rough and smooth towels.
- Pat and wash her body in the bath with washers, sponges, or plastic bath toys.
- Start teaching her warm and cold water.
- Don't forget the hands and feet.

Rolling in a blanket or other material provides sensory input for your infant's brain. Massage is both loving and bonding and helps infants become aware of their body parts. Tell her the body part you are massaging. There are different kinds of massage: deep pressure with the fingers over the body in a regular squeezing motion; light stroking with a soft brush or fabric; tapping or rolling a ball or other objects.

Touch experiences inside and out

Sensory experiences are important. Try these:

- swinging in blankets
- rolling down slopes

- the feel of different surfaces: prickly or soft grass, paths, sand, dirt
- the smell of flowers

MASSAGE, EXERCISES, MUSIC

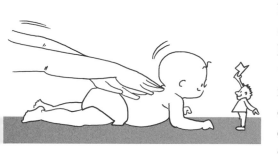

Massage should be without clothing, but this is not always possible. Infants do not feel the cold as adults do. Despite your baby's preference to be "on the go," try to get her to lie on her front for massage and mix it up with exercises. You need to be firm and quick! Provide interesting noisy or squeaky toys or mirrors.

Talk during massage and exercise

- Talk lovingly or sing rhythmically while you massage and exercise your infant.

- Don't forget her hands and fingers, feet and toes.

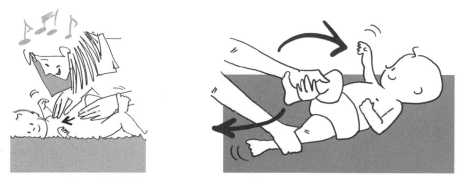

- Hands and feet are important. Leave your infant's feet bare whenever possible. The sensations through her feet match up and work with her eyes to develop balance.
- For listening experience, play hide-and-seek with sounds or music. Can she hear where the sound is coming from? A turn of her head will tell you. Music can be soothing, relaxing, and stimulating and can even affect moods.
- Be happy—your feelings are contagious!

TUMMY TIME

Do not encourage your infant to sit up—she will usually sit up of her own accord after she has been crocodile crawling or creeping for a time, once adequate muscle tone has developed. This avoids any postural problems.

Tummy time is also an important stage for near point vision and visual adjustments as infants look around.

Tummy time activities

Encourage your infant to be on her front, looking at a toy or book, going to investigate a noise or looking at herself in a mirror.

Infants who develop good motor skills have learned about their world from many positive and negative movement experiences. This helps protect them against serious accidents—they are fast learners!

Rocking
Infants love being rocked over a big therapy or beach ball, on their fronts or backs—all ways.

Take care of your infants while doing these activities.

CRAWLING ON THE FRONT

Brain development hinges on interplay between the genes you are born with and your experiences. Early experiences help to shape and form the brain. Crawling on the front is one of the most important stages in brain development.

- Some infants crawl early, others later. Nature dictates when an infant needs extra time before creeping. Often it is a result of the lack of tummy time and muscle tone development. It has nothing to do with intelligence.
- Infants who commando crawl will usually creep. Cruising around the furniture follows. Let them cruise and creep—do not walk them.
- Intellectually, early walkers are not smarter than those who walk later.

Crocodile change and crawl forward

Initially this forward movement is one-sided, then the other, and even both hands and both feet, but it soon becomes perfect. Cross-pattern change movement (now called commando) later becomes cross-pattern crawl forward.

Exploration stimulation

There is a vital period of development when infants move across different surfaces, giving their senses more opportunities to hear, see, and taste the properties of everything as they move around. Infants love this period, for at last they are moving!

Pots and pans make great noises

Kitchen cupboards are magnets for this age group (see page 39).
Think of the great sensory stimulation they provide!

BOTTOM SHUFFLERS

Tummy time is great brain stimulation for all infants. Some infants become bottom shufflers and miss the creeping stage, especially those who are sat early. Bottom shuffling is often avoided by not propping your infant in the sitting position. No infant should be sitting until the protective reflexes develop in the latter part of the first year, to stop them from falling. These reflex actions are connected to visual adaptations in varying positions. All infants must develop these balance reflexes in order for the interconnections in their brain to grow.

You can nurture your child's development by providing daily opportunities for her to enjoy and participate in development activities, which help infants to overcome the need to bottom shuffle.

Stairs

Going up and down stairs is an excellent way of getting bottom shufflers to perform the creeping movement.

Obstacle courses

Going over obstacles to get a toy (as this graphic shows) often challenges a bottom shuffler to find another way over!

Infants who bottom shuffle eventually walk and catch up the sensory motor stimulation they missed. However, not going through the normal developmental movements is a gamble in relation to learning abilities, but not a health hazard.

SHOULDERS, ARMS, AND HANDS DEVELOPMENT

Development and behavior can be affected by the food available today. If you have questions concerning your child's behavior or development, seek professional advice from specialists who will listen to you.

Row, row, row your boat . . .
Encourage the infant to hold a little bar or hold your hand over hers while gently pulling her back and forth to a song such as "Row, row, row your boat." Encourage bending of her elbows to strengthen the muscle tone. Note the hand to help lower the head if necessary.

- The hands are an extension of the arms and shoulders. If the muscles in the arms are poor, the handgrip will be weak.
- Hold your infant's head if there is any head lag. This is often due to insufficient tummy time.
- Try more tummy time over a low roll or cushion.

Wheelbarrow
Lay the infant on her front, holding her around the hips, then lift her up onto her hands. Encourage her to walk on her hands, while singing—
Everybody rolling, rolling, rolling,
Everybody rolling just like (Jane).

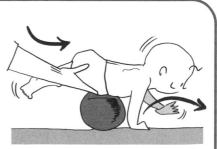

Rolling your infant back and forth over a small ball helps to prepare her for hand walking, if her arms are not yet strong enough.
Watch for hands flat on the floor.

BALANCE THROUGH MUSCLE TONE STIMULATION

In infancy, balance movements must be repetitive for the pathways in the brain to develop. Note the effect that muscle tone has on balance. Children with poor muscle tone often have extra difficulties. The balance reflexes are also developed and stimulated through the vestibular system (inner ear). For this reason, vestibular activities are vital in all programs in this book. Always protect the head and neck when doing vestibular activities.

Games on the roll, therapy or beach ball, or parents' legs help strengthen hand/eye connections, as well as leg, knee, and foot development through muscle tone stimulation. Such activities prepare the infant for sitting and creeping, and eventually cruising and standing. Do not sit or stand your infant before she can do it herself. Infants crawl, sit, creep, cruise, stand, and finally walk when their muscle tone is adequate and their sideways balance reflexes have developed. These are not primitive reflexes, but postural ones that stay for life.

Balance

Sit infant on the roll while it is moved backward and forward slowly and gently, or straddling the roll, or side to side for balance and footwork. This strengthens tummy and back muscles, to help provide balance.

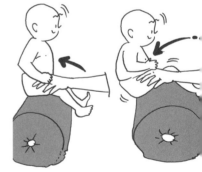

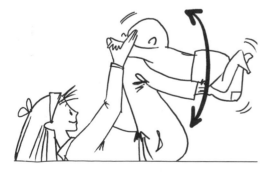

Flying

Lie on your back, with your legs in the air, bent at the knees. The infant lies on your legs, and you hold her arms out as wings and move her legs up and down.

CREEPING ACTIVITIES

Creeping is a vital stage for sensory stimulation, muscle tone, and visual development. The distance between the creeping baby's eyes and hand will be her reading distance at school. Think of the increase in focusing and the muscular adjustments of the eyes as the infant moves different distances to and away from toys.

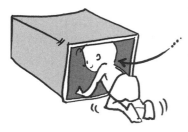

Space awareness

Creeping under and through chairs and tables is great for space awareness. They see a toy and "quick as a wink" get it! Make an obstacle course of chairs, stools, and cardboard boxes for your baby.

Slope fun

Look for hills and slopes in your area. Maybe make one in your backyard or in the playroom. Creeping up slopes and rolling down is fun.

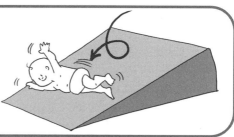

Creeping balance

Creeping along a raised surface is a challenge. Your infant will enjoy going across it many times. This activity requires visual awareness of depth.

- Creeping follows crawling on the front, and is another important period for sensory motor development.
- Infants learn about space fast: Will I fit? How long will it take me to get that toy?
- Infants become cross-patterned (left knee and right hand moving together) for balance, laying tracks in the brain for later development.

LADDERS

Ladders are a fascination once infants are mobile. By ten months or earlier, infants learn to lift their leg to get it over the rung, as they grasp the next one up. Watch that the hand is full grip with the thumb under the rung.

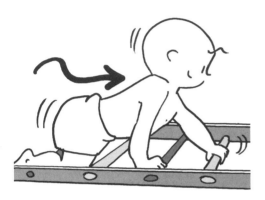 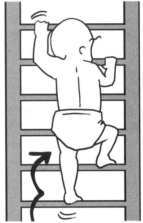

Creeping along ladder rungs

Encourage the infant to move along on hands and knees or feet. Painted rungs help color awareness. Correct handhold of the rung, with the thumb underneath, creates a good pencil grip later.

Climbing a perpendicular ladder

Perpendicular ladders are the easiest to learn to climb. It is like creeping upward. Help your infant to get her feet on the rungs, and the hands, too, if necessary.

- Repetition brings learning.
- Provide a short baby ladder, with twelve rungs of ¾-inch dowelling, 4 inches apart. This will develop the handgrip and increase muscle tone, as the infant pushes upward or along to reach the next rung.
- Placing her foot in the right position requires her brain to work as she forges new pathways, strengthening the co-contraction in her knees for later bobbing, then jumping.

CRUISING, BOBBING, AND THINKING

Creeping, standing, and cruising are all the result of primitive reflexes. When the head looks down, the legs straighten and the arms bend, but when the head looks up, the arms straighten and the legs bend! Soon infants begin to cruise around furniture as they learn to cope with standing against gravity. When cruising, they are not walking.

Standing and cruising
Remember, your toddler is not walking. Do not encourage walking by holding your baby's hand.

Bobbing
To cruise, infants have to bend at the knees. Placing objects on the floor causes your infant to get down (bob) from upright, and up again. Think of the muscle development this requires.

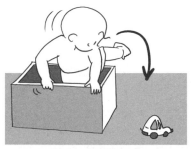

Getting out of a box
Infants and boxes go together. Look at the motor planning required as the infant works out how to get out of the box to get that toy car.

Standing upright and cruising does not mean your toddler is walking. Give infants time to strengthen their legs for later free walking. Months of important creeping are still to come before infants walk independently. Early walking, unless preceded by five months of crawling and creeping, is an "at risk" factor for later learning difficulties.

EXERCISES: 10–12 MONTHS

When doing pull-ups, infants may need help to grasp the stick. Hold your hands over theirs as they pull up. If their muscle tone is slack, "tease" the arms a little to stimulate the muscle tone and do not pull the infant right up.

Consider earlier activities for the muscle tone development of arms and legs, along with rhymes and songs.

Pull-ups
Try pull-ups, with your infant grasping a rhythm stick or rings, to improve muscle tone development in the elbow. The correct handhold is a full handgrip with the thumb underneath.

Following simple commands
Clapping hands, banging objects together, and shaking rattles are great activities and can be done on command to music, to stimulate developing rhythm.

"Look what I can do!"
Practicing a one-foot exercise while holding on!

Your infant is entering the bilateral stage where both sides of the body work together doing the same thing. Infants are now learning to anticipate actions, but letting go at the right time is often difficult, so encourage and don't force this new release skill.

DANCING

- The vestibular system, balance, and vision are interdependent.
- These activities are loved by all—rhythmic, fun, and developmental!
- By ten months they can be a little more strenuous.
- They are wonderful for visualization.

Dance (1)

Bouncing and jiggling. Hold the infant around the waist, provided her head control is good. If head control is still a bit weak, stay with the earlier holds, supporting the head and neck area.

(2) Spin from side to side and around.

(3) Swing up and down.

(4) Repeat these activities, or put in your own steps, such as a waltz.

- If the infant is too heavy or you are ill or pregnant, do not attempt lifting activities.
- Vestibular stimulation helps the development of muscle tone and is important to all gross motor functions.
- Muscle tone and muscle strength are different. Muscle tone is not voluntary and is a brain function dependent on sensory motor input. Muscle strength can be voluntarily improved through fitness programs to reduce the fat to lean body mass.

ROCKING, SWINGING, AND JIGGLING

- Rhythm is essential to language, development, and learning. Even mathematics requires rhythmic abilities, in order to sequence.
- Most primitive reflexes are overcome through vestibular stimulation and massage.
- The following activities are very important for normal, balanced development.

Riding

Sit with your infant on your knees facing you, holding hands. Jiggle and joggle the baby while chanting:

This is the way the ladies ride (jiggle slowly)
This is the way the farmers ride (faster)
This is the way the gentlemen ride (faster still)

The jiggeddy jog is created by the parent raising one knee at a time at the varying speeds.

- Every infant should have a toddler swing.
- All activities mentioned earlier that involve rolling, tumbling, spinning, swinging, or rocking are not just fun, but increase your infant's developmental capabilities.
- Think of the messages to the brain while your little one is swinging or spinning gently around. Even the eye muscles have to work!

Toddler swing

Swing or spin gently. Once she can sit herself up, this is a firm favorite.

Rocking

Sit with your legs extended on the floor. Place the infant on your legs with slightly raised knees, then rock back so she is almost standing on your stomach. She sits on your lap as you rock back and forth.

VISUALIZATION

Visualization is the ability to remember the look, feel, smell, or taste of things—such as a pattern of movement, or a sequence of sounds.

Visual tracking & focusing

Tracking a ball or toy also involves visual convergence. Move the toy around, up, down, and across, near and far. As the infant gets near the toy, the two eyes learn to focus at differing distances.

Visualization—posting

Posting is both enjoyable and compulsive, as nature insists on getting this eye/hand coordination right! When things go out of sight, infants also learn they do not disappear.
Where are they?

Word visualization

On an 8 x 8-inch white card, write a word (lowercase) with a black marker. Prepare up to seven words, and flash them four times daily. Each day replace an old card with a new one. Get your child to match the word card to a picture card. Don't ask what the word is; just show the card and say the word. This will enable her to visualize words as she learns to speak. Make it fun!

Remember: do not show the picture and the word on the same card!

- All activities in this stage of development create visual stimulation as the infant moves around.
- Visualization is also experienced as more situations and movement abilities are developed. Visualization develops from sensory experiences.
- Environmental situations differ. Some infants become familiar with pets. Some live in the country and others in the city. Most have sight, but some do not and rely on other sensory inputs.

STAGE C: WALKING TO 18 MONTHS

This is the bilateral stage, when both sides of the brain learn to work together.

Motor abilities are so important that speech takes a backseat. The age a child walks is less important than the sensory motor stimulation he receives from tummy time, crawling, creeping (for about five months), cruising (as he adapts to the upright position), then walking unaided.

With improved balance infants begin to bob, run, and refine their gross and fine coordination skills. When your child begins walking without assistance, walk with him as often as possible, first on flat ground, then up and down slopes and then running, which at first is really a slow walk. Make it a game to see how far and how fast your toddler can walk each day.

Note: Use toddler reins where there is danger. Don't drive or use a stroller if your toddler can walk the distance with safety.

MASSAGE, MUSIC, AND SONGS

- This is the "runaway" stage of your infant's life, so massaging is not easy. Do it at diaper change time, in the bath, or while nursing him across your knees, and talk to him as you massage.
- Baths are calming and are a good time for body massage and relaxation of muscles and ligaments.
- Use different things for massaging, not forgetting rough and smooth towels.
- Massage and exercises must be done slowly so the messages from the muscles and ligaments have time to register in the brain.
- Sing rhythmically as you move their limbs.

Arms across the midline

This exercise is to be done slowly. With your infant on your lap, stretch his arms up, down, out and in, firmly—but do not force. Then cross his arms over his body and cuddle, first left over right, then right over left arms. Repeat several times.

Legs across the midline

Lift one leg up across his body to the nose and back, then the other leg.
Repeat several times, then do alternate legs up to the ear or cheek.

These exercises are for massage, body awareness, and muscle and ligament stimulation. Be sure to fully extend the limbs, out and across, but do not force any movement. Sing and move to a rhythm.

BASIC MOTOR PLANNING: 12–15 MONTHS

Motor planning is the ability to program a movement in sequence. The following activities are forging the first steps in this process.

Fun in the family room

Allow your toddlers to have fun playing on some furniture. Remember, through play they are learning how to move their bodies through space, as they clamber up, over, and down the furniture.

Walking over the rungs of a ladder

Ask your toddler to lift his leg over the rungs of a ladder lying on the floor, while holding on to the rung ahead. Now raise the ladder on books or low chairs and repeat the activity. Increase the level of difficulty, because this activity is important.

BOOKS

It takes motor planning and environmental experiences to know when to lift that foot to get over or up on to the ladder rung, when to hold on to (or let go) that bar, and why you have to creep to go under chairs. These activities create sequential pathways in the brain, which, after much repetition, become automatic.

Creeping through ladder rungs and under chairs

Creeping forward through the rungs of a ladder on its side, or under chairs, requires many senses working together. Space awareness is developing fast. Watch for hands flat on the floor with thumbs out.

BALANCE: 15–18 MONTHS

- This is a movement year and although language begins, it usually takes a backseat.
- Use language in relation to ongoing events, otherwise it is just noise.
- Help your toddler's balance by walking with him as often as possible, first on flat ground, then on different surfaces such as sand and dirt.

The feet and eyes must learn to send the same messages to the brain about their position. If this does not happen, balance is affected. This skill needs repeated experiences, as it is during this year that this matching occurs in the brain. The child should have bare feet, so make your room warm enough. Colds are not caught through the feet.

Hills and slopes

Provide hills and slopes for your toddler. At first he will use his arms excessively for balance. Support him if necessary, holding him lightly from behind—under the elbows of outstretched arms if walking up a slope. As balance improves, he will learn to run fast and bob to play. Bobbing develops the muscle tone in the legs, knees, and hips. This muscle tone often needs to last for eighty years or more!

Walking backward/sideways

This requires balance and body/space awareness. Initially help, but then let your toddler try for himself. Encourage walking sideways, walking backward, and crouching. This is important for gaining visual adjustments.

DEVELOPMENTAL ACTIVITIES: 15–18 MONTHS

- Treat any discomfort in your toddler's ears seriously.
- Diet can be a major trigger for ear infections. Intolerance to specific foods can cause earache.
- Ear infections can affect language as they interfere with interpretations of sounds and words.

Topsy-turvy

Stand alongside your squatting toddler, then lean over and put your left arm under and around his waist.

Place your right hand on his head, which goes down and slightly under, then roll him over. Make sure your hand follows through, so that his head is protected.

Try it with a rag doll first!

Parachute reflex over a ball

Lay your toddler on his front across a large roll or big ball.

His parachute reflex will cause his arms to go forward to the floor as he rolls forward.

Check his head is against the ball, so that when you roll the ball forward he will do a somersault over the ball.

Your infant will soon tumble himself, so teach him the right way. The head should be well under. It is important that the head and neck are supported as he is turned over in the somersault. These activities must be done on a soft mat.

UPPER BODY DEVELOPMENT: 15–18 MONTHS

A safe commercial trapeze bar is an investment in your child's future. Hang it securely *inside* so that you can use it regardless of the weather. Be sure to place a tumble mat underneath.

Rocking

"Row, row, row your boat . . ."
Parent and toddler sit opposite and hold hands, as they rock back and forth. The child should keep his body straight as he goes backward, and elbows bent as he goes forward. Rock no more than five times.

Monkey swing

Toddler swings like a monkey holding on to two rings. If necessary, help him to hang by putting your hands over his.

This activity activates chest expansion and deep breathing.

Throwing requires timing (temporal awareness) to know when to release the ball. At this age, the ball is often released too early. Rocking and hanging by the hands increases muscle tone in the elbows, which strengthens neck muscles. Poor muscle tone in the shoulders, elbows, and hands can cause writing problems later.

Throwing

With your child standing up, ask him to hold a big ball up very high with straight arms and throw it to you.

VESTIBULAR STIMULATION

Research has shown that the growth of the pathways in the brain is, in part, the result of vestibular stimulation. As movement activities stimulate the vestibular system, they influence body and space awareness, muscle tone, and the adjustment needed by the eye muscles for corrected vision. The vestibular system (inner ear) has a strong influence on muscle tone, which is at the core of most developmental and/or learning disorders.

Ball or roll balance

With your toddler sitting on a long roll, lift his legs a little, creating a forward balance movement.
Move the roll back and forward to stimulate the balance reflexes.

Scooter board riding and spinning

Lay your toddler on his front on a scooter board, with his legs straight out behind and head up. Take care to ensure his hands are holding the edge of the board to prevent his fingers being rolled on by the wheels.
Push and spin him around slowly.

Spinning can be done on a swivel chair, but it's recommended that you buy a scooter board. They look simple, but commercial ones are better than home-made ones! They are not skateboards and must never be stood on or used without supervision.

ROLLING AND TIPPING BACKWARD

Vestibular stimulating activities are vital for toddlers' hearing, speech, and vision.

Beach ball stretch

Lay your toddler on his back over a big therapy or beach ball, with his arms stretched back overhead to reach the floor. Stretch forward and back, then sideways.

These activities stimulate the vestibular system, which influences body and space awareness, muscle tone, and also the adjustment needed by the eye muscles for corrected vision.

Respect his response. If it is hurting or frightening him, stop and check for ear infections and try a more gentle approach, such as over a chair.

The parachute reflex occurs when your toddler goes upside down, and his arms go downward to protect the head! These reflexes are automatic and stay for life.

Tipping downward

Hold your infant as he sits with his legs around your waist.

Then lean forward so that he is partly upside down.

Support the back of the head, neck, and upper back.

ROCKIN' AND ROLLIN'

Rocking and rolling

Lay your toddler on your thighs,
holding his hands.
Then rock with him, back and forth.
Aim to get into a rhythm with a song like
"Everybody rocking, rocking, rocking."

- Vestibular stimulation is important for hearing, the ability to listen, and helping overcome any remnants of the primitive reflexes.
- Listening is vital in developing the visualization skills needed for learning.
- Songs from different cultures also keep the ears alive.
- Learning a foreign language is very beneficial both intellectually and for brain development.

Pencil rolling

Lay your toddler sideways
on your legs with his
hands straight overhead
and legs down straight,
like a pencil.
Roll him over and over
down between your legs,
along the floor between
two people, or down a
slope, ending up with him
on his front for a massage!

Do not worry if the legs and arms are not straight when rolling over at this age. Some body parts are still a bit of a mystery.

MUSIC, RHYTHM, AND SONG

Early stimulation of your child's hearing is essential to his understanding and language development. For musical activities, all you need is the two of you and your voices. Your infant won't care if you're not a good singer, so just try! Your obvious pleasure will pass on happy feelings. Attitudes are caught, not taught.

Nursery rhymes and songs

Bounce and sway your infant on your knees, as you sing or act out nursery rhymes and songs.
Stamp your feet while singing,

Baa baa, black sheep, have you any wool?
Yes sir, yes sir, three bags full.
One for the master and one for the dame,
And one for the little boy who lives down the lane.

Try lightly tapping your infant as you invent or recite nursery rhymes.

- Rhythm is a part of every gesture.
- Musical toys can be fun! Banging pots is developing rhythm. Make simple homemade instruments, as suggested earlier.
- Music is special for infants. Hearing experiences help develop and expand intellectual potential. Just as food nourishes an infant's growing body, so the elements of music, melody, tone, and harmony nourish his rapidly developing brain.

Maracas

Give your toddler a pair of maracas (or a rattle, bell, or drum) to shake in response to the beat of well-known play songs or nursery rhymes, and suggest some word patterns as an accompaniment, e.g., children's names: "Da-vid" (two beats), "Tif-fa-ny" (three beats), "John" (one beat).

DANCE EXERCISES

The circuitry in the brain between music and mathematics is connected. Stimulation of these connections is essential at all ages, as rhythm aids sequential memory for mathematics and motor planning.

Dance
Walk your toddler to the beat of the music, stopping every so often to:
• Bob up and down.
• Do "ticktocks" from side to side with him standing on your feet.
• Rock from foot to foot (one-foot balance).
• Hold him under his arms and swing him.
There are many similar activities described in this book for each stage of development.

Bobbing is important for developing the knee muscle tone for walking, climbing, and raising the knees to get over obstacles, going upstairs, and clambering onto furniture and other objects. Dancing, then freezing, then dancing again helps stimulate the rhythms. If your child is not free-walking, lift him up. It is not helping your infant's development to force him to be a toddler. Let your infant develop at his own pace.

VISION

Visual tracking and adjustment to varying distances are important side benefits of all ball and balloon games.

Hitting a balloon with a fly swatter

Show your child how to hit a hanging balloon back and forth by hand—first one hand, then the other.

Then show him how to hit the balloon with a fly swatter, with your help.

Try chasing a balloon.

Roll the ball

Sit or kneel opposite your child. Roll an 8-inch ball between you.

All ball games require visual adjustment between the two eyes as they follow the ball, as well as the motor skill of letting go of an object at the right time!

Parachute ideas

Make a parachute with a soft material. Play hide-and-seek as you push the parachute upward. Shake and watch it as the balloons go "up, up, up," then "down, down, down"—then give teddy a go!

- Toddlers notice everything within their personal space, and everything they see they want!
- They are perpetual motion machines and love to spin until they fall down.
- Nerve messages from the inner ear affect eye muscles and are vital to visual development.
- A common visual difficulty at school age is adjusting vision from far to near point.

VISUALIZATION

- Listening skills help in the development of visualization.
- Reading or looking at books with animals and objects with which your toddler is familiar is very important.
- Movement helps dramatically in visualization skills. Doing is learning through visualization experience.

Familiar pictures and books

Every day read books and flash "word" cards and "picture" cards showing familiar animals and objects for your toddler to visualize. (Remember: one page for the picture and one page for the card.) Gradually introduce extra words like "big" and "little." Make a scrapbook of pictures of places your toddler has visited recently, such as the zoo, beach, park, train, or shopping mall. Read these with him. This also develops speech!

Visualization is happening all the time through your toddler's movements. Just look at what he is visualizing as he shakes his rattle to a nursery rhyme.

Most adult readers read via visualization, which has developed over years of reading. This skill develops pathways in the brain through experience. It is an essential skill for motor planning, which begins in infancy. Visualization is an important aspect of behavior. We learn by cause and effect. This is not well developed in young children!

STAGE D: 18–24 MONTHS

During this period many toddlers are still in the bilateral stage of one-year-olds. Bilateral means that both sides of the body do the same thing. The brain has two sides or hemispheres. The left side controls the right side of the body and the right hemisphere the left side! During this stage, infants use both sides together, doing the same thing as in riding the scooter along, or finger painting, where they will frequently use either or both hands, depending on which side of the body the object they want is lying.

Note: **Definite handedness is rarely developed before 2½ years of age and should not be forced.**

During this bilateral period, infants practice their existing actions and controls, thereby improving, consolidating, and perfecting them. Infants refine their movements with repetitions, so that the network of nerves in the brain works more efficiently. Bobbing stimulates the muscles needed for the new skill of jumping—a milestone for the two-year-old! Awareness of space and how to move the limbs in coordination with the arms and balance needs lots of practice as the nerve pathways in the brain are laid down.

MASSAGE

Lay your toddler on her front on the floor or across your lap, while you play massage games on her back. Sing to her. If she complains, stop and change your form of massage.

Front massage

Using tapping and light rubbing, massage the face, head, chest, stomach, legs, and arms. Use one kind of massage each session. Make up a rhyme or sing while you massage.

Back massage

With your toddler on her front, massage to a weather theme. For light rain, use long smooth strokes; for heavy rain, thunder, and lightning, use different appropriate strokes.

When your infant is 20 months old, try putting her into the crocodile position (see illustration). Do this in stages: first her legs, later her arms and lastly her head!

Touch gives us a sense of reality; not just body awareness, but even what exists outside us is based on touch. Children need a lot of touch sensations to develop the emotional and social stability needed for independence.

MASSAGE THROUGH EXERCISE AND SONG

- Nodding, swaying with the whole body, bending, bobbing, and bouncing are fun—and they also provide important messages to the brain to stimulate rhythm in movement, which helps coordination.
- During massage, name each body part as you touch it.

By 20 months some toddlers can move their limbs in and out together by themselves, while others still need help with these activities.
Repetitive movements and songs strengthen the neural pathways from the brain's thinking area to the motor areas and out to the nerves that move the muscles, providing excellent muscle and ligament massage.

Water play

Children love water play. It does not have to be in the bath.

A portable tub with various containers for squeezing, spraying, and pouring are great.

Hickory, Dickory, Dock

Nursery rhymes can be used for massage.
Run your fingers over your child's body like a mouse, but do not tickle her. Bounce her on your knees while you recite:

"*Hickory, Dickory, Dock,* (jog child on outstretched legs)
the mouse ran up the clock, (raise your knees)
the clock struck one, (give a slight jolt)
the mouse ran down, (lower your knees)
Hickory, Dickory, Dock." (jog on your knees)

There are other movement and play songs that create feelings in the muscles and ligaments. Do at least one each day.

EXERCISE TO MUSIC

- Matching movement to speech helps children move rhythmically and helps link thoughts and actions.
- You will still need to help your toddler with these exercises.

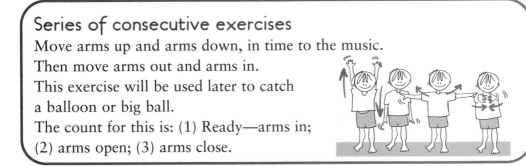

These activities coordinate the body with the brain by linking internal motion with the external sounds of music. They also enhance internal recognition of rate, rhythm, and time, and help develop muscle tone, flexibility, and gross motor coordination.

Series of consecutive exercises

Move arms up and arms down, in time to the music.
Then move arms out and arms in.
This exercise will be used later to catch
a balloon or big ball.
The count for this is: (1) Ready—arms in;
(2) arms open; (3) arms close.

Song with actions

Facing your child, who should be standing with her
feet apart, sing and point to the relevant body part:

Head, shoulders, knees, and toes,
Knees and toes, knees, and toes,
Heads, shoulders, knees, and toes,
We all clap hands together.

Stop and make sure your toddler finds her head
(count 1), shoulders (count 2), knees (count 3), and
toes (count 4), before continuing.
Do this slowly as many cannot do it fast.
Help is often required. Repeat several times.
Vary body parts according to abilities.
Try this action song with a beanbag or rhythm sticks.

NURSERY RHYME MOVEMENTS

All cultures have nursery rhymes and songs for young children. Below are two common English nursery songs.

Make up rhyming ditties about daily happenings. Repeat the songs many times. Your toddler may join you with sounds or odd words. Later, leave off the last word and your toddler may say the word or at least make an appropriate sound.

Jack and Jill

Jack and Jill went up the hill
To fetch a pail of water,
Jack fell down
And broke his crown
And Jill came tumbling after.

Sit the child on your outstretched legs.
Raise your knees and bounce her.
Let her go gently to the floor
between your knees.
Roll her down your straightened legs.

Nursery rhyme CDs are made for preschoolers and are too fast for toddlers and even some three-year-olds. But they are still important for neurological development, so you need to learn the songs and sing them slowly for your child.

Rocking all about like a boat on the sea

Rocking all about
like a boat on the sea,
Rock, rock, rock, rock,
Rock along with me.

Rock toddler back and forth on a medium-sized ball, trampoline, bed, or roll.

MUSCLE TONE DEVELOPMENT

- As your toddler gains more control of her body, experimenting with motor actions is possible.
- Promote listening by whispering to gain her attention.
- Resist loud talking and yelling to gain your toddler's attention unless there is danger.

Movement exploration is a great way for toddlers to learn about themselves and their world, as new pathways are forged in the brain. Make sure adequate space is provided for free movement and safety. Arms should now not usually be required for primary balance.

Hanging by the hands
Hold out two rings for your toddler to hold on to, making sure that her thumbs are underneath. Then gently and slowly lift her off the floor briefly. Put your hand over hers if her grip is weak.

Climbing
Your toddler will climb anything—furniture is great fun! Watch that her handgrip is the full hand grasp, with the thumb underneath.
Guide, but do not help unless necessary!

UPPER BODY DEVELOPMENT

Provide a horizontal ladder with six rungs, 9 inches apart, or a trapeze bar for your toddler to hang from, or you may find your towel rail in the bathroom broken. Place tumble mats underneath when the bar is in use.

Hand-walking and hanging are fun. For heavy toddlers, use a broom handle held between two people. Put the broom handle ends on the shoulders of two adults, who hold the handle on their shoulders with one hand and the other hand over the toddler swinging from the bar. Hand-walking strengthens hands, arms, trunk and abdominal muscles, while gross and fine motor development are also stimulated. Hold your toddler at the hips, or lower down the legs if she can maintain straight legs. She may sag and be unable to do this if her muscle tone is not yet adequately developed.

Hanging from a bar or rings

Children of this age love to swing by their hands from a short bar. Watch the grip (fingers over the bar, thumb under), and hold your hand over theirs until they can grip it themselves. At first, lift them up by the bar briefly, only for as long as your toddler can hold.

Wheelbarrows

First, hand-walk along the floor as before, then try hand-walking along a wide beam.

Then raise the beam slightly.

ANIMAL LOCOMOTION

- Stopping and starting help stimulate the rhythm for keeping the beat in movement, and for forming phrases in speech and thinking.
- These actions also stimulate balance and help the child respond to sudden commands, needed in dangerous situations.
- Animal songs are wonderful for free movement by children.
- These activities also aid the vital skill of visualization, as children pretend to be specific animals.

Dog or lion

Ask your child to choose to be a cat, dog, horse, mouse, or lion.
Get her to make the animal sound and move around at different speeds.
Watch that her hands are flat on the floor.

Elephant

An elephant goes like this and that,
He's terribly big and he's terribly fat.
He has no fingers, and he has no toes,
But goodness gracious, what a nose!

This year, toddlers are trying to get both sides of their brains to work together, in preparation for their next stage, when the two sides learn to do different actions, and the top and bottom halves of their body can also do different things, such as riding a tricycle or being an elephant.

VESTIBULAR BENDING AND SPINNING

- Hugging helps to connect the body with the brain by linking internal motion to the external sounds of music.
- Your child is now slowly mastering the rhythms of music. Try slowing down the action, but still keep the rhythm.
- Spinning slowly is an important activity that helps override a primitive reflex.

Hugging body parts

This activity is to promote crossing the middle of the child's body in preparation for further brain development.

Have your child stand with legs astride and arms at her sides. Then ask her to step forward with the left foot, bend at the waist, and hug the extended leg with both arms, to the count of four. Repeat with the other leg. Repeat the exercise five times.

Spinning

Sit on a spinning chair with your child on your lap. Spin the chair slowly, five times to the left, then five times to the right— thirty seconds to each rotation. Before each rotation, stop and touch five body spots, telling her where each place is located. Her eyes will be open as children at this age can rarely shut their eyes voluntarily.

All exercises must be done according to the capability of your toddler. If she does not like a specific exercise, it could be that she can't do it, or it hurts her ears, especially the spinning. Try something less stressful!

WHEELBARROWS, SWINGING, AND SPINNING

Trapeze bars are a must for older toddlers and children of school age and above. They love to hang and spin. You can buy one commercially, or make one with strong dowelling, tied securely with thick nylon cord. Place a foam mat underneath.

More stimulation is given to the muscle and ligament nerve center when activities are done slowly. This age is a great time for multisensory stimulation to the brain in preparation for the major development of integration, when all the sensory inputs come together in the brain. These activities provide excellent vestibular stimulation.

Wheelbarrows

Hold your toddler by her lower thighs, and hand-walk her across the room. If she has difficulty taking the weight on her hands, hold her farther up her body. Her body and legs should be straight.

Try hand-walking her along a wide balance beam or up a ramp, ending with a tip-over! Make sure her head is well under.

Swinging and spinning

Try swinging and slow-spinning your child in a toddler swing, hammock, or blanket, or slow-spinning on a swivel chair.

BALANCE

- Balance is an automatic function dependent on the adequate inhibition of the infant reflexes.
- Holding the toddler's hand during an action experience requiring balance is counterproductive to her balance development, as the parent is balancing for her!

Kicking and balancing on one foot

Ask your toddler to stand on one foot with the other foot balanced on a ball. Then try the other foot. Then shuffle or kick the ball forward.

Steps

Provide a few steps for your toddler to learn to climb stairs.

Jumping into a hoop

By 22 months of age, some toddlers are jumping so well that they can jump into a hoop, or over an object such as a rope, with good balance.

Imbalance creates balance. Toddlers may creep up steps at first, but as balance improves they will step with one foot and then the other on the same step. Independent walking up stairs (i.e., one foot to a step) develops later for most toddlers. Talking and balancing at the same time are still rare.

FURTHER BALANCE

- Balance and muscle tone develop through movement.
- Balance requires muscle tone and body awareness, in order to balance one side of the body against the other.
- Stimulation through vestibular activities should precede balance activities.

Large ball play

Lay your toddler on her front over a 25½-inch therapy ball. Roll her forward and sideways, then sit her on top of the ball for the same rolling movement.

Walk board

Find a board approximately 7½ inches wide by 6 feet long for your child to walk on. Ask her to hold out her arms placing your hands lightly underneath her elbows for support, ready to grasp if she becomes unbalanced. Ask her to look at an object at eye level at the end of the board, not at her feet, as she walks along the board.

The upright stance is the product of the earlier primitive and balance reflexes developed through repeated movement during the first months of life. These reflexes have resulted in the development of muscle tone, body and space awareness, and tactile, visual, and auditory skills, all required to maintain the upright body position. Balance and posture are necessary for coordination and later motor development.

RHYTHM BAND

Time and rhythm are interdependent. Rhythms are patterns of movement coordinated to produce fluent movement. Without this, there is dysrhythmia (lack of rhythm). Rate, rhythm, and time are known as temporal awareness. Children with rhythmical difficulties find changes in routine difficult.

Rhythm

There are many ways to provide rhythmic sessions with your toddler. Homemade instruments such as rice in plastic bottles to shake, two rhythm sticks (dowelling 9 inches long, .87-inch diameter, with nontoxic painted ends for color awareness), rattles, saucepans, and wooden spoons on upturned ice cream containers make great sounds!

Play or sing tunes with varying speeds and beats: slow, fast, and some that stop every so often.

Rhythm sticks and maracas

Rhythm sticks and maracas are great for beating time on the floor, together or individually. Bang up high, down low, and on body parts. Copy patterns with 4 or 5 sticks each, and use different colors, too. Tap the sticks together in different ways—hard and soft.

Have older children join the fun and, through visualization, pretend they are a big band!

At this age, help your child to do two things at once. Tapping, clapping, and chanting children's songs and nursery rhymes all help harmonize the child's body movements, due to their effect on the vestibular system.

MOTOR PLANNING THROUGH DANCE

- Basic motor planning involves motor skills.
- Emotions can be portrayed in dance.
- Structured rhythmic movements enhance motor planning and sensory stimulation.
- Free dancing is an excellent option.

Motor planning and sequencing are still not well developed. Only do sequences of two or three different actions per dance. If you give your child more commands than her age, she will probably not be able to remember them and may only do the last request.

Dance variations

Circle dance: Holding hands, run or walk around in a circle for eight beats. Stop. At each stop do an activity, two to three per dance, such as bobbing or stamping.

Walk four steps into the middle and four steps out, forward and backward. Taking little steps and big steps is a challenge.

Clap or stamp, slow and fast, four times.

On tiptoe, stretch hands up to be tall.

Try circling without holding hands. Stop. Stamp on the spot, clap, or tap body parts.

Hold partner's hands, go around in a small circle, then bob and jump up.

Run around with the child on the ground, or a big spin if she is not too heavy. (Children this age often spin themselves.)

Repeat the circle dance.

This is excellent vestibular stimulation, but do not lift your child for any activity if you have a bad back.

SENSORY MOTOR PERCEPTUAL ACTIVITIES

Sensory motor activities lead to perceptual abilities, as the brain makes sense of what the child has experienced through movement. Toddlers are very inquisitive. Nothing is safe as they move around, touching, smelling, eating (sometimes), listening, and feeling everything in their environment.

As earlier skills are strengthened, new nerve growth enables new abilities to develop.

The brain controls the muscles, and the ability of the brain to send clear signals to its muscles depends on correct functioning and movement experiences.

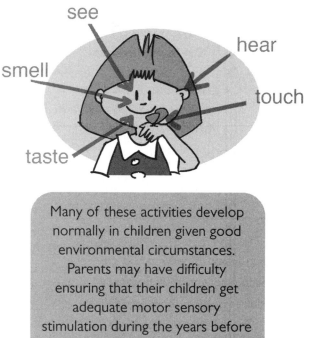

see

hear

smell

touch

taste

brain

muscle

"It is important to note that all communication skills, reading, writing, speech, and gesturing are motor based." (Jack Capon, founder of Perceptual Motor programs)

Many of these activities develop normally in children given good environmental circumstances. Parents may have difficulty ensuring that their children get adequate motor sensory stimulation during the years before school age, due to environmental situations and lack of parental awareness of the value of sensory motor perceptual activities. School readiness develops and strengthens during the years before school age.

B: Writing requires fine motor coordination, which develops as a direct result of adequate velopment of all sensory functions—especially gross motor coordination.

BEANBAGS AND BALLOONS

- Beanbags and balloons are excellent for motor movements and temporal awareness of rate, rhythm, and timing.
- "When should I release that beanbag, so it goes where I want it to?" Toddlers need to learn how and when.
- To provide color experience, use red, blue, green, yellow, white, and black beanbags.

Balloon throw and catch

Hold the balloon with two hands and throw it up into the air. Can you catch it?

With arms out to the side, close the gate (arms come in) to catch the balloon.

Beanbag pass and release

Pass the beanbag from hand to hand. Always say the color of the bag.

The aim is to release the bag. Can they drop it a few inches?

Basic motor planning, fine motor skills, and body part awareness are stimulated in the above activities. Dropping the beanbag (above right) at the right time is difficult, but regular practice will create strong pathways in the brain so that it will happen.

BALLS

- All children love balls, small or large.
- Rolling them and running to catch them is fun.
- Few toddlers are able to hit them with a fly swatter; even balloons are not easy to hit.
- Sometimes a ball can be caught in a hug.
- You need balls of all sizes, preferably soft blow-up balls or foam. Hard balls can hurt.
- Repeat all activities many times!

Rolling and small bounces

Sit facing your child. She rolls or bounces the ball to you with both hands, several times. Then ask her to do it with one hand, then the other.
Roll the ball back to her.

Motor planning with balls

Get your child to stand up and throw a tennis ball–sized foam ball. A small ball will probably result in the use of one hand—the one nearest the ball! Encourage her to throw overhand— suggest she touches her ear with the ball before throwing it. Either hand will do. Then use the other hand.

Ball play is excellent for temporal awareness development. Throwing involves the brain sending messages to the relevant muscles and ligaments to release the ball at the right time! This requires developmental motor skills and hand/eye coordination. It is a difficult time, as children rarely have a preferred hand at this age and can't cross their midline, so they throw with either hand, depending on which side of the body the ball is placed.

HOOPS

- Hoops can be purchased from toy shops and department stores.
- End each session rolling the hoop.

Most 1–2-year-olds only remember one or maybe two requests. If your child has difficulty jumping, don't ask her to jump. Remember that no matter how many times you ask her, she will forget what you asked, while trying to remember how to jump! Either help or ask the child to do something they can do! Children's development varies.

Concept development with hoops

Ask your toddler to:

a. Sit in the middle of the hoop on the floor.
   Lift the hoop up high, then low to the ground.

b. Stand up, walk around the inside of the hoop.
   Walk around your hoop, one foot inside and the other foot outside.

c. Walk forward, then backward, around the hoop.
d. Stand in the center of the hoop on the floor.
   Rock from foot to foot (ticktocks).
e. Stand beside the hoop.
   Step sideways into the hoop and out.
Repeat each activity three to four times.

RIBBONS AND CORDS

- These activities are primarily for balance development.
- Use six colored ribbons, each six or seven feet long, and a skipping rope. Colors should be red, blue, yellow, green, white, and black. Matching colors comes before naming them.
- Repeat each activity five times.

Walking on the ribbons

Place one or two colored ribbons, stretched out straight, in front of the toddler. Then ask her to:
Walk on the ribbons to the end, turn around, and walk back again. Can she walk heel to toe?
Walk up the ribbons with one foot either side.
Walk sideways along the ribbons.
Jump up the ribbons and back again, with one foot either side.
(For older children who can jump.)

Creeping along the ribbons

Ask your toddler to creep like a tiger up and down the ribbons on her hands and knees. Now creep like a bear up and back on the cord. Bears creep on their feet—left foot with left hand, then right foot with right hand.

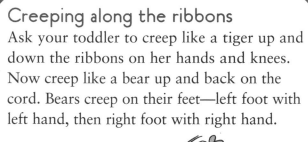

Provide help, praise, and hugs if appropriate. Remember, your toddler may not have been walking for long! Repetitions are important for good stimulation of the brain pathways. Finally, name the colors you use for color awareness.

VISUAL TRACKING

- Visual tracking activities promote a toddler's ability to follow moving objects.
- Experience is the key to vision, through stimulation of the five senses.
- Taste is still necessary for visual development. Note how toddlers love to taste everything!
- All movement activities stimulate visual development.

Visual tracking

Any rolling game provides lots of visual tracking and coordination.

Ping-Pong balls being rolled around inside hoops on the ground may keep toddlers watching briefly!

Rolling balls along the ground or around, in and out of things, with rolled paper or cardboard rolls, is chaotic fun.

Try visual tracking, one eye at a time.

Then try both eyes tracking an object—preferably with as little head movement as possible.

Flashlight tracking

Play a flashlight beam on the ceiling in the dark and ask your toddler to follow the light on the ceiling, then you follow the light!

Ask your toddler to shine the light on objects in the room, then follow the light across the room *without moving her head*. There are many variations.

Many people have poor visual perception—they see but do not always understand. This can lead to reading and learning difficulties. It is the stimulation of all our senses that promotes visual perceptual abilities.

VISUALIZATION

- Visualization is the ability to remember a pattern of movement, a sequence of sounds, and the look and feel of things. It is an important tool for learning.
- Toddlers' drawings are still mainly up-and-down strokes and circles drawn with either hand. These improve along with their body awareness and visualization skills.
- Picture books suddenly become firm favorites.

Picture books and photo albums

Collect photos or drawings of objects familiar to your child to make a special scrapbook. Talk about what you see. Does it make a noise? Read lots of picture and short storybooks. Re-read her favorites again and again to provide bonding, visualization, and language awareness.

Copying people and objects

At this age "pretending" is a favorite activity. This is visualization and should be encouraged. Dressing up is a firm favorite. So is imitating your pet animal or someone in your home, or doing "cooking" or "gardening," or being a car or a train. All are excellent for visualization development.

People who can "see" in their minds specific sentences in a book have a great ability to visualize. Adults read via visualization, which has been acquired through constant exposure. It is an essential skill for motor planning, which begins in infancy.

STAGE E: 2–2½ YEARS

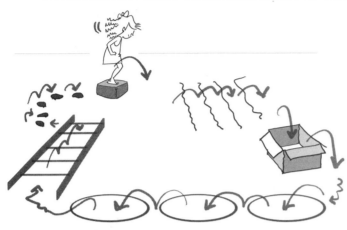

Refinement of posture and balance occurs during this period, as body and space awareness improves. The integration of sensory information that flows into our brain makes it possible for the brain to fine-tune its responses, and improved motor planning begins.

This stage is followed by increased perception and laterality.

The balance and coordination of your child is very important. If you have any concerns at all, it is a gamble to do nothing. A little help may prevent many difficulties in later years. Regardless of any developmental "hiccups," remember that your child still has intelligence: the brain just needs the right stimulation. If you buy an expensive computer and do not install the right software, it does not work very well, if at all!

This can be a difficult behavioral stage. Do not spoil your child. Do not become a victim of infant tyranny. Stick strictly to a routine, especially in relation to diet! Cause and effect is well and truly established by this stage. Burton White, a child development specialist and founder of "Parents as Teachers," tells us that infants learn to manipulate their parents from approximately five months of age!

MASSAGE IN CROCODILE POSITION

- The aim of combining crocodiles with massage is to help the child understand that this position means massage and songs, which they usually like!
- Aim for a slow, coordinated, fluent change—head, arm, and leg all changing together.

Massage time

Lay your child in the crocodile position and massage him as you did at earlier stages.

Try to position him as shown in the illustration.

Talk about the "straight side" and "bent side" while massaging.

Then change sides and repeat.

Crocodile (alternate one side)/change, then crawl forward.

Change *homolateral* (one side) position from side to side slowly, assisting initially. This must become a coordinated movement as (all together) the arm slides down, the head turns, and the leg bends up, while watching the thumb of the bent arm as it comes up opposite the nose. Repeat this movement five times.

For maximum sensory input to the brain, do this as slowly as possible, with approximately two changes per minute. Sing or say rhymes, or count.

When it's safe to do so, let your child go barefoot to provide feeling through the feet. Eyes and feet work together for balance. The crocodile position helps to ensure that the primitive reflexes of infancy are no longer affecting his co-ordination. This specific movement develops body awareness, motor planning, muscle tone development, and visual and auditory pathways.

ANGELS IN THE SAND

Research has shown the nonstimulated brain has fewer neural pathways than the stimulated brain. Sensory integration is just beginning, and the child is starting to understand the concepts of right and left.

Angels in the sand

This is an old exercise, wonderful for body awareness, left and right awareness, and later cross-patterning.

The child lies on his back on the floor like a pencil and moves his arms and legs slowly in, out, up, down, individually or together, to the beat of music, as you instruct him.

Now tell him to move his arm and leg on one side *slowly* up into the bent position—sideways. Watch the thumb of the bent arm as it moves up slowly to eye level and back again. Then do the same on the other side. Repeat this five times.

Finally, try cross-pattern actions—for example, ask him to move his right arm slowly along the ground and above his head, while he moves his left leg out sideways.

"Angels in the sand" exercises can be done to music occasionally but are best done very slowly to enable the pathways in the brain to develop fully. Remember, only one or two commands at a time. These exercises develop muscle tone, body and space awareness, fine motor skills, gross motor skills, and motor concepts.

BODY AWARENESS AND VESTIBULAR STIMULATION

Exercises make pathways in the brain that need reinforcing during these early formative years.

Rocking and rolling

Lying on his front, rolling and rocking back and forth on a 8-inch medium-sized ball is excellent vestibular stimulation. Sitting on the ball and bouncing is developmental fun.

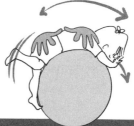

- By adding rhymes to exercises you are adding memory and rhythm work as children learn by rote.
- Pretending to be an animal like a frog is great for visualization—be sure they have seen a frog or a picture of one.
- Jumping like a frog provides excellent muscle tone development.
- Ensure that the child bends his knees as he bounces. For those not yet jumping well, "Jack in the box" is a great prelude to jumping. It is also great vestibular stimulation for all little ones.

a. Jack in the box

Get your child to follow the cues as you say:
Jack is quiet down in his box,
Until someone opens the lid!

b. Frog jumps

While you say this rhyme, the child squats, placing his hands flat on the mat between his legs, then springs forward like a frog.
Mr. Frog jumped out of the pond one day
and found himself in the rain.
Said he, "I'll get wet, and I might catch a cold,"
so he jumped in the pond again.

ROLLING AND TUMBLING

Vestibular stimulation should be done for only two minutes, followed by a static exercise, as the nerve endings tire and are no longer stimulated. It's similar to having your palm tickled—at first it feels great, but after a while there are no good feelings.

You will need a tumbling mat or old foam mattress for these exercises.

Tumbling and rolling over and over provide massive stimulation, as the fluid in the inner ear rolls over the nerve endings, which send messages to the brain about what is happening so that the eye muscles can adjust accordingly.

Rolling up and down in a rug

Roll your child in a rug, ensuring that his head is not enclosed in it. Pull one end and unroll him. He will roll over and over as you tip the rug up and down. Ask him to try to keep his body straight. Try this activity with your child holding a ball overhead.

Tumbling

Teach your toddler how to tumble, so that he does not hurt his neck. The safe way is:
a. bob down
b. bottom up and head well under
c. over you go.
Ask him to do five tumbles down the tumble mat.

SWINGING AND SPINNING

- Objections to vestibular activities are frequently due to ear infections. Watch your child's eyes after he spins. If the vestibular is underachieving, then his eyes will not be moving back and forth. This is typical of an overactive child.
- Spinning must be slow and controlled for nerve growth stimulation in the brain. Rapid spinning is fun and should be allowed as play only. Remember that after two minutes the nerve endings tire, so limit the time you spin your child for maximum stimulation.

Jump box

Stand your child on a small box. His knees should be slightly bent, arms back. As he jumps forward into the hoop, his arms swing forward.

Step and jump over a rope

Ask your child to step or jump over a low rope slung between two chairs. Start with the rope on the floor and gradually raise it until it's about 2 inches off the floor.

Spinning

Spinning can be done on a hanging tire, scooter board, office chair, or similar equipment. The toddler lies in the swing tire and is spun *slowly*, one revolution every thirty seconds. Stop after each revolution for five seconds, touching and naming five different body parts, then reverse spin. Repeat.

This can be a difficult period for your toddler: one minute he thinks he is grown up, then he reverts to being an infant. A toddler swing may not be acceptable! Improvise with a rope swing fixed firmly from an overhead beam—but not outside, as it will be unusable in bad weather. Use a scooter board if nothing else is available.

WOBBLE BOARD AND BALANCE BEAM

Always support your child if his balance is poor—but just do so lightly under the elbows from behind. Avoid holding his hands, as this means you are doing the balancing.

Wobble board

A wobble board should be ½-inch plywood or ¾-inch pine, 14 inches square.

Place under the center a block of timber 3½ inches square, 1¼–1¾ inches thick, with rounded or angled edges.

Sit your child in the middle of the board so it is balanced. Provide help if necessary.

Then show him how to pass a beanbag from one hand to the other. This helps him realize he has two sides and teaches him how to balance one against the other.

Walking on a balance beam

Balance beam: 3½ x 1¾ x 71 inches.

The child walks forward and with his right hand drops a beanbag into a container on his left. Then, still walking the beam, he drops a beanbag with his left hand into a container on the right side. He should have bare feet for stability.

Safe balance develops along with control of your body in space. Remember, balance is developed through imbalance. Postural control is achieved through signals from the brain, which has received messages from the vestibular and visual systems, and from muscles and ligaments about the body's position.

MOTOR PLANNING: DANCE

Children motor plan as they play and dance. Without the sensory skills to develop body awareness, balance, and the integrating pathways in the brain, many common daily actions such as walking up steps, dressing, and knowing hot from cold, are difficult.

All young children love repetition. Use music with a good beat. Slowly develop a sequence for your child to remember.

Simple basic circle dance

Start with two different actions and if this is managed, add another. For example: spin around, jump back and forth, alternate  foot rock, clap hands with partner, spin around. The aim is to keep the rhythm and beat as the child memorizes the sequence of actions.

Motor planning is initially conscious, but with repetition and practice it becomes automatic. Moving the limbs slowly requires motor planning control. Movement to rhythm is enhanced. These activities are vital for inhibiting the primitive reflexes. Dancing creates awareness of body and space, as the child avoids bumping others.

Line dance
Parent and child face each other. Move toward each other, then back: four steps in, four steps back. Do an activity when you meet in the middle. Keep the four-beat rhythm.

MUSIC, RHYTHM, NURSERY RHYMES, AND SONGS

- Rhythm and music are essential for smooth coordination.
- Rhythm is also important for the development of visualization and language skills.

Singing and acting animals is fun. Remember to keep the beat.
Some children are hypersensitive to noise, so keep the music quiet.
As food nourishes the body, so music nourishes the brain through melody, tone, and harmony.

Farm, zoo, or beach song

I went to visit a [farm / zoo / other place visited] one day
and saw a cow along the way,
and what do you think I heard her say?
Moo, moo, moo.

This song can be used anywhere there are animals for a child to imitate.

Humpty Dumpty

Humpty Dumpty sat on a wall . . .
Sit on the floor with your child sitting on your raised knees. Then straighten your legs so he falls down, then jiggle him.
Try other nursery rhymes or songs of your country.

RHYTHM STICKS

- Rhythm sticks provide exercises to integrate sensory and motor neurons. They are used with children under two, mainly as bangers on upturned ice cream containers.
- Exploring movement through rhythm sticks creates a positive sense of self.
- Color code your rhythm sticks as you do your beanbags.

Body awareness

Seat your child in front of you, and on your instruction get him to tap both sticks gently on body parts to the beat of the music.

Sometimes one stick will cross his midline, and sometimes two sticks. This requires the parent to "accent" the beat.

Rhythm sticks and basic concepts

Instruct your child to bang his two sticks up in the air, down low, in front, behind, to the right side, and to the left side. Tell your child which is left and right.

Then vary the game with sticks to toes on one side, then cross-pattern (see page 10).

Repeat both of the above activities with one stick, then the other.

Many of these suggestions are challenging, and you may need to assist your child to understand some of the concepts involved, such as up high, over your head, in front of the body, under the knees, and keeping the beat. These activities help the development of hand/eye coordination and develop listening skills and concentration. Rhythm sticks also stimulate eyesight, hearing, touch, and feeling from the muscles and tendons to activate interconnections within the brain.

BEANBAGS

Children of this age can do many things with beanbags. They can be used as stepping-stones, jumped over, thrown at targets—overarm or underarm—and placed on body parts. They may also be used for cross-patterning: the child stands or sits with legs apart, and with the beanbag in the right hand leans across the body to touch the left foot. Then with the beanbag in the left hand, touch the right foot. Do color-matching whenever appropriate.

Repeat any two of these activities two to five times per session.

Beanbag balance

Can your child jump over your beanbag, forward, backward, and sideways?

Ask him to hold a beanbag between his knees, then his elbows. Can he walk or jump without dropping the beanbag?

Ask him to put the beanbag on one foot. How far can he kick it? Now try with the other foot.

Concepts with beanbags

Sit the child down and place a beanbag on his head. Ask him to tip his head forward to drop it onto the floor in front, then backward to drop it behind, then forward into his hands. Repeat the exercise standing up.

Beanbag play promotes body awareness, balance, color recognition, and hand/eye coordination. Beanbags are very versatile!

BALLS

Balls are excellent for helping the brain to forge pathways and guide the child into advanced skills, such as throwing and catching. Initially this will be a hug catch (arms open wide, then "shut the gate" so the arms come in to catch the bigger ball), and later they will catch with their hands.

Repeat activities two to five times.

Concepts and balance with the ball

Can your child stand in front of the ball? Now ask him to turn around to face the ball. Can he put one foot on the ball for two minutes, then the other foot?

Ask him to kick the ball gently with one foot, then the other.

Through ball play, children learn about concepts, balance, visual adjustments, and space and body awareness. With the two sides of the brain beginning to work together better, they are starting to catch and throw with one hand, though still often with the hand nearest to the ball! Their hand/eye coordination improves through repetition of a variety of activities. Integration is on the way, along with the development of a preferred hand.

Ball bouncing

Standing up, can he bounce the ball down on to the floor? Ask him to open his arms wide (gates opening and closing), then close his arms on the ball as it bounces up to him. Practice this a few times.

HOOPS

**Hoops provide an excellent medium for motor development.
Repeat these activities two to five times.**

Motor planning with hoops

Place the hoops in different patterns on the floor
and ask the child to jump—step—jump—step
down the line of hoops. If he is not yet jumping,
then step only.
Advanced: Jump through three hoops, straddle jump
the next two, jump, turn around, and return.

Hoop rolling

Roll the hoop, pushing it
on its edge across the room
to the child, who rolls it
back to you. Show him
how to push the hoop with
a flat hand on the top.

Remember—this age can usually cope with only one or two instructions.
A child may seem incompetent, not because he can't do the task, but
because there are too many instructions for him to remember. If so, step
back to an easier task. Make sure you allow for variation in abilities in
relation to sequences in motor planning. Slowly, through repetition, the
pathways in the brain develop.

RIBBONS AND CORDS

- This is a reinforcement of actions done with hoops at an earlier stage.
- Ribbons should be in six colors, the same as beanbags and rhythm sticks: red, blue, green, yellow, white, and black.
- The cords are fun for tug-of-war (great for muscle tone) and animal tails!
- Every touch sensation will enhance the development of nerve pathways.
- Repeat each activity two to five times.

Concepts with ribbons and cords

Get the child to place the red ribbon in a straight line, then:

a. Place it *in front* of, then *behind*, himself, then *in front* of, and *behind*, you.

b. Make a circle with the cord and stand *inside* the circle, then *outside*.

c. Snake-wiggle the green ribbon *in front* of, then *behind*, himself, then *in front* of and *behind*, you.

d. Place the cord *around* your waist and be a horse to pull him, then change over so he is the horse.

e. Get him to crawl on his front *under* a cord, then jump *over* it, *backward* and *forward*.

Play matching and naming colors with beanbags and ribbons.

NB: Cords must be used under supervision and put away out of reach when not in use.

These activities also promote color awareness, coordination, and flexibility and provide opportunities for creative uses, such as tying boxes together to make a train.

VISION

Vision is involved in every movement. Every time you say "look," you are helping your child refine his visual processing.

Eye tracking must not last more than one minute for each eye. While awake, children spend hours unconsciously inspecting their surroundings. They love to watch flickering lights, as these stimulate vision. In the past this occurred at the fireside; today twinkling toys have the same effect.

Far point visual tracking

Hold a favorite toy at full arm distance from your child.

Play the game "Can you follow the toy?" (put toy behind your back).

It's disappeared—here it is dancing around in a circle, back and forth and in a vertical cross.

Can he catch it?

Near point visual tracking

Hang a favorite toy or ball at the child's eye level and ask him to follow it visually at a child's shoulder-to-hand distance. Use alternate hands to hit the toy.
Clap a slow beat.

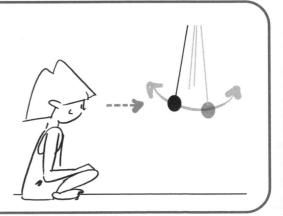

VISUALIZATION

This is the age of copying someone in the home. **Children cannot yet draw anything recognizable, but as their visualization and motor skills improve, so do their drawings, and their visual memory of word cards and picture cards.**

Visual memory

Every day ask your child something about what you did the previous day. Maybe you went on a train or car ride, or visited a farm and saw some chickens.

Ask your child: "What did you see?"

Prompt if necessary and congratulate him for helping you to "remember."

Children cannot visualize what they have not seen. Visualization is the language of the processing of thought, along with the messages received by the brain from all the senses (touch, smell, taste, hearing, and sight) and emotional feelings. Children of all ages love free movement as they become fairies or animals they have seen. It is a time for creativity and pretending (visualizing).

Visits

Take your child to the museum, art gallery, park, zoo, beach, or other place of note. Collect items to put into a scrapbook about the visit. Put the item on one page, and the word on the opposite page (one word 1¼ inches high, as large print is easier to perceive than small) so the child can picture the visit in his mind while he looks.

Do not show the picture page and word page together.

Remember—read the whole word quickly (do not sound it out).

STAGE F: 2½–3½ YEARS

This exciting stage of *integration* and *laterality* development is the result of a spurt in brain development. Many children enter this age a toddler and emerge as a child. It is when awareness of others and recognition of things in the past can be remembered!

Vision has almost fully developed as they move around in space with great fluency and confidence. It is a time of sensory *integration*, when the brain puts together and uses information received from the ears, eyes, skin, nose, tongue, muscles, and joints to make sense. This is called perception. With a good supply of sensory information, the two sides of the brain get their act together, so that both sides of the body can work independently. This is called *laterality*. Body awareness now can include the right and left sides.

Children can now do different actions with each leg and also their arms, which enables them to do such things as riding a tricycle—one leg down, one leg up, and different actions with their arms. Fine motor tasks now explode; each hand can do something different like cutting out, where one hand holds the paper while the other cuts.

If this level of brain function is not yet developed, both hands will try to do the same thing.

Remember: It is not whether a child can do these activities, but the intensity, frequency, and duration at which they are done.

MASSAGE IN CROCODILE POSITION

Play soft, relaxing, rhythmic music. Recite rhymes or sing songs they love, to encourage memory and language—rote learning is vital. All actions must now be done very slowly, to increase sensory input to the brain.

Remember: Intensity, frequency, and duration are the keys to maximum sensory stimulation.

Crocodile change and forward movement

First massage in the crocodile position, do several changes, then get your child to push forward, one side at a time, with the palm of the bent arm flat, and toes of the bent leg underneath for traction. Then swoosh her back by her feet.

Watch that there is no overflow of movement on the other side of the body—especially the foot. Repeat the side changes (not the forward movement) on her back—slowly.

Use a slippery surface for ease.

Commando movements are important as they continue to increase muscle tone and play a vital role in the sensory developmental areas of the brain. The same action on the back helps to ensure that an important reflex is inhibited.

Commando (cross-pattern) change and forward movement

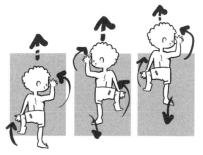

In the crocodile position, change the legs only, so the bent leg is on the opposite side to the bent arm (cross-pattern). Her straight arm should be on her buttock, and her head facing the bent arm. Change from side to side.

Continue until the head, arms, and legs move together, then ask her to roll over and do arm and leg changes in a stationary position on her back. When this has been achieved, she should try a forward cross-pattern movement.

TIGER CREEPING

Creeping on all fours is a motor stage of further *integration* of the primitive reflexes and sensory stimulation. Slow speed, accuracy of action, smoothness, repetition, and a coordinated, rhythmic beat are important both forward and backward.

Forward

The child needs to be on her hands and knees, with her hands a shoulder-width apart.

She then lifts the left hand and right knee together, with the right knee landing behind the right hand. Then the right hand and left knee do the same as the tiger moves forward. She should lift the knees but drag the foot with toes stretched out behind. Her hands should be palm down on the floor with fingers together, thumbs out. When she's ready, ask her to turn her head from side to side to look at the forward hand.

To create resistance: Kneel and hold the child at the ankles, keeping her feet on the floor.

- A "Go" signal gives the child time to initiate the movement before she encounters resistance.
- Resistance stimulates muscle tone, as well as stimulating the sensory system.
- Creeping is a good time to do rote learning—for example, days of the week, even short nonsense rhymes. This causes thinking while moving (a skill required in spelling) and is excellent for laying down a memory tract in the brain.

Backward

Place your hands on the child's buttocks, keeping your arms straight. Then ask her to creep back, pushing you *backward*. Get her to look up at a target, to counter the effect of an earlier reflex that gets infants up on all fours in infancy.

FINGER AWARENESS

Finger skills are important in almost every walk of life. The nerve endings in the fingertips are *very* sensitive. All activities that use the shoulders, arms, and hands are strengthening the fingers.

- Studies of children's motor achievements and characteristics show that they are affected by experience.
- Exercises should now be performed in correct detail, with frequency, intensity, and duration, in order to ensure that the appropriate nerve pathways in the brain are adequately reinforced. As adults know, it is hard to change the way we do something.
- By the age of four, most children will draw people with a body, due to increased body awareness.

Finger development

For all activities involving the hands on the floor, ensure that they are palm down flat with fingers together and thumbs out. When grasping the rungs of the ladder, ensure that the grip is overhand with the thumb underneath.

Finger painting

Finger painting allows for full development from the shoulders to the fingers. It might be a mess, but it's great for finger development—and it's fun!

Buy nonpoisonous finger paint. Provide a large piece of wet butcher's paper, a flat table, a smock, and a blob of finger paint for your preschooler to swish across his midline as he draws or makes swirls.

MINI-TRAMPOLINE EXERCISES

- Do bouncing exercises on a mini-trampoline, an old spring mattress, or the floor!
- To stop, your child must bend her knees and put her hands straight out in front of her.
- Never have more than one child bouncing on a rebounder or trampoline, unless their hands are being held.

Bouncing

Try actions on the floor first, including the stop movements.

Bouncing is a series of little jumps. Many children have difficulty doing a single bounce in one movement to each count—they double-bounce instead. Do it slowly on the floor to correct this—it sometimes takes lots of practice.

Ask your child to bounce five times, then stop. Repeat, giving a different number of bounces, with a stop in between.

If successful, give two or three commands sequentially.

Bouncing and turning

Ask your child to swing her right hand up, back and around, and at the same time jump a quarter-turn to the right. Repeat this until she has done a full turn.

Repeat with the left arm swinging to the left.

Put a sticker on the back of her right hand for guidance if necessary.

Concepts are learned through commands for movement activities. Bouncing is vestibular stimulation—do not overdo it. Give instructions according to your child's ability to succeed! Children develop at different rates.

BODY AWARENESS AND CONCEPTS

Body awareness and concepts continue to be the key to both physical and mental development. Body parts, planes, laterality, and directionality are learned progressively throughout childhood. Until a child can interact successfully with her environment in ways that are meaningful and fulfilling, accurate body knowledge and a positive body image must be developed.

Body awareness and concept revision
The child stands for exercises in slow motion, using all previous concepts, such as hands up above, below, in front, behind, and beside her body parts, as well as ticktocks, rocking, hopping, jumping, running, and turning.

It is important to reinforce these new abilities, such as crossing the middle (midline) of the body, jumping confidently, standing on one leg and (for some) hopping, and all the common conceptual words. Right and left awareness is just beginning, but can be enhanced through repetition.

Fun body awareness game
Instruct your child to touch different body parts on command. Can she do this with her eyes shut? Use left and right commands for crossing her midline (e.g., right hand on left shoulder). At this age children are still learning their left and right, so you may need a sticker on one body side.

Ask your child to touch one body part with another, such as hands to shoulders, or hands to toes.

Also ask her to touch parts of the room, such as putting her ear to the wall, or her right hand to the door.

SPINNING AND SWINGING

These activities are part of playtime for most children, but need repetition through a daily program of exercises for three to five minutes, a vestibular exercise for two minutes, and massage, repeated once. Early in the morning is the best time.

Remember: *Good, better, best,*
never let it rest,
until your good is better
and your better, best!

Slow spinning
Sing:
Look at me, I'm spinning, spinning, spinning,
Look at me, I'm spinning, round and round I go.

Swinging by hands
All children love to swing, so put up a trapeze bar for your child to swing and spin.

Encourage leg-lifting, by hanging a balloon for her to kick as she swings.

- These vestibular activities should be part of your small daily program. Do one of them each day, along with a balance, massage, and crocodile activity.
- Vestibular activities are important for all ages, and only change in accordance with the age and skills of the child.
- Ensure the vestibular activities stimulate the fluid in the inner ears on different planes—up and down, from one side to the other. This can be done by having your child spin in different positions on the scooter board, spinning chair, or slippery floor!

ANIMAL BALANCE POSITIONS

Balance skills are essential in order for integration and laterality to develop. Animal walks and funny poses are excellent for balance stimulation. Children of this age love to copy animals. Read lots of picture books to your child and point out different animals. Take them to the zoo.

Animal positions

While you count to five or ten, ask your child to pose like a:

a. four-legged animal.

b. lame dog on three legs (two hands and one leg).

c. bear squatting (hands outside the knees).

d. seagull on one leg (arms crossed).

e. kangaroo standing ready to jump (arms out in front, as you bob down and up).

Up and down steps

Ask your child to go up a flight of steps . . . and down again.

- A demonstration may be necessary, as the verbal instructions may be too complicated.
- Balance is a vital skill and must occur before one-sidedness can be established.

WOBBLE BOARD

- Laterality is preceded by integration (the ability to move the body in a coordinated manner), and is totally dependent on the development of balance and posture.
- Junior wobble boards are available at most toy or sports stores—or make one.

Remember that balance is created by imbalance, as the body flexes the limbs alternately until balance between the two sides is achieved. Balance increases the awareness of the two body sides, left and right, helping the child attain laterality.

Balance on the wobble board

Child places her feet either side of the center of the board and balances in this position.
a. She sits with arms out sideways as she tips from left to right ten times.
b. She sits with arms crossed as she tips from side to side ten times.

Balance activities

Once balance is obtained, see if she can catch a soft medium-sized ball five times, and/or hit a balloon alternately with the right, then the left hand.

LATERALITY FOR 3-YEAR-OLDS

- Laterality can only be developed on the foundation of good balance.
- All activities for laterality must be preceded by one or two balance stimulation activities.

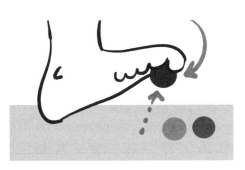

Picking up marbles by the feet

This is a fun game to play with one child or a group. Child picks up marbles one by one with her preferred foot and places them on the other side of a piece of string. How many marbles can she pick up with her toes? Allow one minute for each foot.

Right and left on the rebounder

Reinforce earlier rebounder activities with this age group, turning to right and left on the mini-trampoline. Most 3-year-olds will now prefer either left or right, so all turns should be to the preferred side. You can now issue a sequence of three or four instructions, such as "Jump six times, stop, turn to your preferred side, stop, jump six times." Only go as far as your child can manage.

These activities are excellent for the development of laterality and an awareness of right and left body sides. Sequential memory requires much practice. Make sure your child is not frustrated—she must be successful. Success breeds success!

CROSS-PATTERN MOVEMENTS

- The standard upright cross-pattern movement is: the right arm and left foot go forward, then the left arm and right foot. This is seen in normal balanced walking, running, throwing, and other similar activities.
- Walk your child every day and go a little farther each week. Ensure she swings her arms in cross-pattern! Start timing how long it takes to go a specific distance.

Crocodile/commando forward movements

Tiger creep: The child needs to be on her hands and knees with hands shoulder-width apart. She then lifts her left hand and right knee together with the right knee landing behind the right hand. Then the right hand and left knee do the same as the tiger moves forward. Lift the knees, but drag the foot with toes stretched out behind. Hands must be palms down on the floor with fingers together and thumbs out. When possible, ask her to turn her head to look at the forward hand.

These activities help visualizing and memory training. For example, children can recite or sing nursery rhymes, songs, days of the week, months of the year, times tables, and counting while doing crocodile/commando crawling or other appropriate movements. Cross-pattern activities are not possible until integration has occurred within the brain. Integration is the coming together of all sensory messages received by both sides of the brain into one function.

Other developmental cross-pattern activities

Walking
Running
Alternate knee lift and hand tap
Alternate feet touching

Marching
Throwing
Bowling
Crocodile/ commando crawl

MUSIC, DANCE, AND RHYTHM

Lining up behind, in front of or beside another child, taking turns, is helpful when playing or dancing with others. This is an age of independence, so it's time to learn about sharing.

Use appropriate music, flowing and gentle, or crashing waves on the shore for a seaside dance.

Move like an astronaut (or a fish)

A dance of free movement involving visualization of floating in space like an astronaut or swimming in the sea like a fish. Find appropriate music for continuous repetitive dance. At this age, children can begin to cope with this four-beat type of dance, where they sidestep four times, turn around with their partner twice, and sidestep four times again. Repeat four times.

There are books on dances for this age. Movement to music helps to build the important skill of rhythmic movement/coordination and motor planning. Dance also provides a reference library of different sounds—so important to the development of speech and later learning.

Basic dance

The standard dance includes dancing around in a circle, in and out of the center, and some right/left instructions. Help where necessary. Dances relying on right and left awareness such as "The Hokey Pokey," where instructions for left and right body limbs are given, have more meaning now. "Ring-around-the-rosie" and other simple dances also help children to learn to take turns and do a series of movements.

RHYTHM STICKS

Rhythm sticks are easy to manipulate and contribute physically to the development of coordination and strength. Rhythm sticks were introduced in earlier age groups, but mainly as drumsticks. Now older 2-year-olds can learn to do other things with them.

Hand/eye reactions

Child holds a perpendicular rhythm stick with both hands in a full handgrip with thumbs under. Using her fingers, ask her to roll the stick around one way, then the other. Can she now roll two sticks, one in each hand?

Spin one stick on the floor, first one hand, then the other.

Pretend one stick is a hammer and the other stick the nail. Hit the nail stick with the hammer stick, then change hands. Try hammering with eyes open, then closed!

- These activities help develop efficient hand/eye coordination and rhythm. They enhance sensory functioning, particularly vision, hearing, touch, muscle, and ligament awareness.
- Rhythm sticks assure success through a series of movement challenges, and reinforce body rhythm—necessary for good movement coordination.

Listening skills

Tap out a short sound pattern. Can your child copy it? Try two more tapping patterns.

Adjust your patterns so she is successful.

BEANBAGS

These activities stimulate crossing the midline of the body and visual tracking, laterality, balance, and body awareness. They are also fun! Laugh and enjoy them with your child.

- In these activities, the child is interacting with fine and gross motor movements, which reinforce body and space awareness, balance, laterality, and visualization.
- Peripheral vision is what you can see surrounding the target. Children who find it difficult to follow a moving target visually can often catch better when looking at the thrower, *not* at the ball. Encourage them to relax their eyes while looking at a target.

Figure eight

Pass a red beanbag in a figure eight, in and out around your knees—first the right knee, then the left. Then go the other way, left knee first, then right.

Peripheral vision

Child holds a beanbag between her legs, while looking at a fixed object in the room. Try standing on one leg!

Can she toss and catch the beanbag without taking her eyes off the target or catch a beanbag while watching her partner, not the beanbag?

BALLS

Balls of all sizes are now introduced. At this age, ball-handling guidance is given not only to help the normal development of the child in relation to finger awareness, vision, and cross-patterning but also to strengthen the awareness of body parts and how the child can use them to provide more sensory information to the brain for more difficult tasks in the future.

Finger play with balls

Can you hold the ball in front, behind, on your head, and on your wrists with your fingers? Can you hold the ball with only three fingers, then two fingers and finally one finger? Can you turn the ball around with all your fingers?

Body image is important for a child's self-concept, as well as for coordination. Temporal awareness is strengthened by ball play. The cross-pattern bowling stimulates further programming of the two sides of the brain in working together for balance and coordination.

Bowling cross-pattern

Stand opposite your child, who bends her knees and gently bowls the ball cross-pattern, with the left foot forward, while bowling with the right hand. Then ask her to bowl the ball with her left hand, with the right foot forward.

HOOPS

Hoops offer opportunities for new experiences as children experiment by using their new skills to twirl, catch, jump, hop, and use hoops on their body parts.

Hoops and motor sequential planning

Stand in the center of the hoop on the floor on the left foot, then the right foot, to the count of five. Then standing on both feet, bend and pick up the hoop. Hold it around your waist, your neck, above your head, then let it go.

Jump out backward, then jump in, keeping the feet together. Do this five times, then sit down in your hoop.

Long jumps

Jump forward around the hoop on the ground, with one foot inside the hoop and the other outside. Then stand in the hoop and jump out, as far as you can. Land on your feet and stand still (freeze). With another long jump, jump back into the hoop and freeze.

Bob down, put your hands out behind you, then swing your arms forward as you jump out of the hoop.

The child who climbs, experiments with objects such as hoops, rides a tricycle, teeters on a wobble board, tumbles on the carpet, and jumps on the bed has a better chance of good development than the child who sits watching TV.

RIBBONS AND CORDS

- As before, use colored ribbons and sash cord.
- Can your child name the colors yet? If not sure, try matching.
- Repeat all activities five times.

> Activities such as jumping over objects require large muscle contractions, which create further growth within the brain. Motor development cannot be left to chance.

Jumping along a raised cord

Child jumps along a raised cord between two chairs (i.e., one foot on either side of the cord), being careful not to touch the cord. Can she do this backward, walking, then jumping?

With the cord 2–4 mm off the floor, ask her to jump from one side to the other down the cord, then backward along the cord. No touching.

Tiptoe walking and sideways jumping

Get her to walk on tiptoe up and back along the ribbon, arms held out sideways for balance. Then jump up and back along the ribbon from side to side, with a jump around at the end. Try straddle-jumping the ribbon or cord. Can she do this backward?

VISUAL STIMULATION

- Peripheral vision is encouraged by focusing on the surroundings while hitting the ball. This is an important developmental skill.
- Equipment required is a 2-yard length of 4mm cord, a sponge rubber ball, 2¾-inch overhead attachment.

Hanging ball

Allow two minutes for each of these activities:
  a. Child stands and follows the hanging ball visually, across her midline, backward, forward, and around with no head movement.
  b. She hits ball with alternate hands, using full arm swing with knee on the same side being raised up. No head movement.
  c. With head centered, she names objects in her peripheral vision while hitting the ball.
  d. If she is 3 years old, ask her to name the right and left hands as she hits the ball—and raises the opposite knee.
  e. Lower ball to the level of her knees. She then kicks ball with alternate knees.

Creeping and balance, using peripheral vision

Ask your child to get into the creeping position. Extend her right arm forward and left leg backward. Hold for the count of five, while she points to a target with her extended arm, keeping an open peripheral (wide) visual field. Now change over to the opposite arm and leg. Repeat the exercise for five minutes.

If balancing while using peripheral vision is too hard, ask her to stand, point to an object, and tell you what else she sees in the room while looking at the object.

Open peripheral vision is a challenge. These exercises help the child control vision while tracking the ball, being aware of the surroundings and keeping balance.

VISUALIZATION

Children under school age are usually primarily right-brained and learn by whole words. Sounding out words is a left-brain activity, not usually functional until 6–7 years of age. This is a generalization—there are always exceptions! Use words with any number of letters—these are visualization word games.

Matching pictures

Place picture cards (from their scrapbooks if possible) facedown and play "pairs." The aim is for your child to remember the position of the picture and word cards that she turned down. This is a common matching game.

What's missing?

Show the child three–five small toys. Remove one without her seeing, then show the items again. Ask what is missing. A variation of this game is to put the articles in a bag and ask her to find the toy car, for example, by feeling in the bag. Another is to place the toys under a blanket, then blindfold the child, remove one toy, and ask her to tell you what is missing. Put in only three objects at first to make it easy, then add more!

- Visualization is a key to learning. A child learns to remember words, but if the word cannot be put into visual memory, it is forgotten and has to be seen again.
- At this age do not use letter sounds: visualization is the aim. Short three-word sentences can now be flashed. Never flash more than seven cards—put in a new one and take one out each day. Play matching (and similar) games with the old flash cards.

Read, read, and read stories

Run your finger along the lines under the words, and/or ask your child to find a picture she knows in the book.

STAGE G: 3½–4½ YEARS

This stage is the culmination of several years of development during which the child has built up within the brain many neurological pathways through their sensory motor perceptual experiences. It is a "catch-up" time in the area of integration, and a period of *consolidation* of these experiences.

Cooperative play is now very acceptable as older threes gain increased body and space awareness. They have become self-confident and less dependent on their parents—try catching a child of this age! Preschoolers love group play and are beginning to have best friends. Their basic movement skills are at a reasonable level and they are learning to take turns. Movements that were difficult a few months ago are now easy. At this age children love to mimic animals and people in their environment. It is a period of continuing experimentation and joy.

MASSAGE AND CROSS-PATTERN COMMANDO

- Try different types of massage.
- Sing or say rhymes, and cross-pattern change at the end of each rhythmic beat. Soon your child will know many rhymes and begin to say them with you. Rote learning is now easier.

Massage and rolling

With child in cross-pattern commando position on the floor (see illustration), massage his back. Then get him into the pencil position and roll him over and back five times, ending on his back (still in the pencil position). Massage his front, then ask him to do a slow cross-pattern commando change (on his back), turning his head to the same side as his bent arm, to enable the thumb of the hand to be tracked visually as it comes up slowly to the level of his nose. Then he slowly lowers his arm and bent leg and does the same the other side, before pencil-rolling over onto his front into the cross-pattern commando position. Repeat five times.

The crocodile/commando crawl is hard work, but the brain development from the sensations it generates is tremendous.

Crocodile/commando cross-pattern crawl

Ask him to start moving forward in the cross-pattern commando crawl. Aim for controlled, slow, coordinated changes. Be sure the floor is slippery (vinyl works well). Once he reaches the end of the mat, give him a fun pull back by his feet!

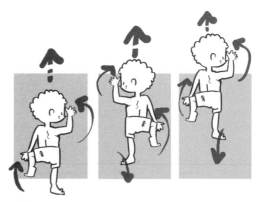

ANGELS IN THE SAND

- The commands in the following activities can be increased as the child gets older, altered by changing the number of times each activity is done, or by instructing the same side or different sides to move individually or together.
- These activities can reinforce movement of limbs without sight and stimulate sequential memory and visualization.

Individual body parts

Give different commands related to moving different body parts, both together, cross-pattern, and individually, such as "move your right foot up and down," "hold your right elbow with your left hand." Repeat all actions three times slowly, counting five seconds in and five seconds out.

Cross-pattern body parts

    a. Right arm and left leg out to the side and back together.
    b. Left arm and right leg out and back.
    c. Right leg straight up in the air and left arm up in the air.
    d. Cross left arm to the right shoulder and bend up right knee.
    e. Cross right arm to left shoulder and bend up left knee.
Again, repeat all actions three times slowly.

Body image is important in the development of a child's self-awareness, as well as coordination. A child needs to know himself as a physical person, and this awareness of the physical body needs to be developed to the highest degree to attain the maximum developmental status.

BALANCE

- Balance activities should follow vestibular activities, and both should precede integration and laterality.
- Riding a three-wheel scooter at this age and a two-wheel scooter at 4½ years of age will enable your child to ride a two-wheel bicycle without trainer wheels when he is 5 years of age.

"Balance control is critical to postural control. Training of these systems is gradual during the development and maturation of the vestibular pathways. Balance begins with the knowledge of one's own position in space. Children who continue to reverse letters, numbers, and words after the age of eight were often found to have immature balance." Sally Goddard, *The Well-Balanced Child*.

Three-wheel scooter

First ride a three-wheel scooter down a slight slope, then between two people, around the room, and finally around a circuit. One foot should be on the scooter with the other pushing.

Hopping

Encourage your child to hop, then skip on one foot, then the other. Hopping requires balance, good muscle tone, and coordination, and will stimulate neurological integration.
Hopping precedes skipping—both essential normal developmental activities.

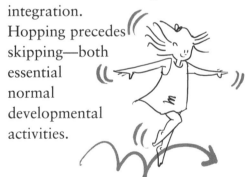

Balance positions
Ask your child to:
a. balance two hands and two feet.
b. balance right hand and left foot.
c. stand on right foot.

SCOOTER BOARDS

Scooter board activities stimulate the vestibular system, balance, muscle tone, body and space awareness, and timing.

Crossing the midline

Sitting on the board, move around with two hands using a rhythm stick as a pole, first on the left side, then on the right. This action helps children cross their midline. To go straight, they change sides alternately. Can your child paddle his way around the house? Spin himself slowly one way, then the other?

Scooter board activities

Lie on the board, legs out straight behind and hands flat on the floor with thumbs out.

Move around obstacles with hands pushing on the floor, then try spinning. Keep eyes open, then eyes shut. All activities are slow.

Appropriate for both school age and younger children who are mobile.

- Encourage head up and legs as straight as possible.
- Scooter boards are good for spinning for all ages.
- Put a cushion on the board to push the child around.
- Scooter boards must be used only under careful supervision.
- Never stand on a scooter board, and always ensure they are upside down when not in use.

MINI-TRAMPOLINE

Mini-trampoline sequencing

Repeat all number sequences six times.

    a. five jumps, stop, seven jumps, stop, four jumps, stop.

    b. four jumps, stop, eight jumps, stop, five jumps, stop.

Make up others for your child's level.

Arm movements

Repeat activities five times.

    Each movement of an arm or leg is done with a jump (just *one* jump per movement—children tend to do two jumps).

    Right arm forward and back, up and down, then same sequence with left arm, stop.

    a. Both arms up and down, stop.

    b. As above with legs individually, stop.

    c. Right arm and right leg forward and back, stop.
       Left arm and right leg forward and back, stop.

    d. Both arms and legs out and in (star jump).

    e. Alternately, one leg forward and other
       leg back.

Midline body cross-overs:

    a. Left hand touch right ear and back, stop.

    b. Right hand touch left ear, and back, stop.

Make up other similar sequences with body parts.

These activities aid both vestibular development and balance and provide sequencing and memory stimulation.

LATERALITY

Through movement, children need to feel that they have two sides to their body, which enables all movements to be balanced. This awareness of right and left sides develops and stabilizes from the use of balance and coordination (posture). An internal awareness of a right and left side is necessary for *laterality*.

From laterality develops a preferred hand, eye, and foot. The child who has not developed laterality often has no preferred side. They are still at the young 3-year-old stage of copying; i.e., if they sit opposite a child at kindergarten who is right-handed, they copy by using their left hand. These children should be checked for developmental "hiccups."

Wobble board

Standing on a wobble board, balance while slow-rocking from one foot to the other, then front to back. Keep arms out straight to the side. Count to five for each leg. Then try catching a medium-sized ball or beanbag while keeping balance.

Midline cross–overs

Standing balanced on the board, the child turns his head and points with the left arm to an object on the right of the board approximately 1 foot away, and then with the right arm to an object on the left side while balancing with the other arm.

DANCE

Dancing to music is excellent for temporal awareness (rhythm, time, rate), body and space awareness, and auditory and visualization experiences.

There are many children's dance CDs. Ensure that your child can follow the instructions—both yours and those on the CD. Music with no voice allows for you to call the instructions.

Dances

Choose a dance CD that is easy, with three or four different commands to follow. Use songs or music such as "Punchinello," "Skip to My Lou," "Clapping Land," "Here We Go Round the Mulberry Bush" and "Looby Lou."

Try activities such as cross-pattern marching, hopping, and jumping backward and forward to the beat of the music. Use sequential commands such as sit down, stand up, stop, start, clap hands, or stamp to the beat five times.

More dances

"I Hear Thunder"
For this dance, the child stands in the center of a room, either alone or opposite a partner. This is a sequential dance done to the beat of the music.

I hear thunder, I hear thunder,	Stamp eight times.
Hark, don't you?	Stand on one leg, hands to ears.
Hark, don't you?	Stand on other leg, hands to ears.
Pitter-patter raindrops,	Tip-toe alternate feet twelve times.
pitter-patter raindrops,	Jump on the spot and shake hands
I'm wet through, I'm wet through.	six times.

Vary the sequence by changing the motor movements, such as marching or hopping instead of jumping.

RHYTHM STICKS FOR 3-YEAR-OLDS

Rhythm or lummi sticks (wooden sticks) are versatile pieces of equipment and available at many toy stores.

To the beat of the music

Your child can be either sitting or standing. Get him to clap two rhythm sticks together, first to the right, then to the left. Place the colored ends of the sticks together in front, then turn them over and hit the other two ends together. Hit them under one knee, then the other (he will need to stand on one leg to do this). Occasionally change the beat for him.

Movement activity with a beat

Thinking and moving together is difficult for many 3-year-olds. Start with beating time while walking. Try stepping to the beat, then change the beat from fast to slow walking. If successful, ask your child to beat the rhythm sticks as they march, first to the right, then the left, up and down, and other ways.

Rhythm in music helps to form patterns of sound. Speech, following auditory instructions, and spelling all require thinking while moving. If right and left are not yet known well, use a sticker on the right hand. Rhythm sticks can be used at any age for hand/eye coordination, general movement coordination, and laterality.

RHYTHM STICKS FOR 4-YEAR-OLDS

Rhythm sticks offer a wide variety of movement skills, moving from the easy to the more challenging skills of rhythm, coordination, dexterity, and balance.

Sound patterns to names and words

Tap friends' names and other words to teach child that all words can be broken into different parts called syllables. He copies the word pattern. Introduce more words as he improves! End this session with tapping to a tune he knows.

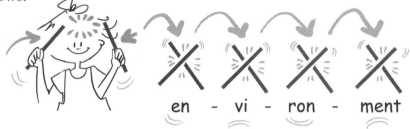

en - vi - ron - ment

Words are made up of syllables, which are really musical rhythmic sequences. Rhythm stick activities help children to hear the beats (syllables). Ask your child to beat out his name. The above activities require thinking while moving! Keep him stimulated, so change the above routine once he has learned to keep the beat. Use kindergarten music—he might even learn the words. This is great memory training; the more of this kind of activity you do, the more numerous the connections in the brain!

Pass the stick

Pass the stick from hand to hand eight times, then around the body twice, changing hands behind the back, then around each leg. End with eight bangs on the floor. Try this with a partner.

BEANBAGS

These activities further stimulate the important sensory input areas of body awareness, cross-pattern movements, concept development, agility, and visual accommodation to varying distances.

Cross-pattern throwing

Child stands with beanbag in preferred hand and prepares to bowl the beanbag. He bowls by swinging the bowling hand backward, at the same time stepping forward with the opposite leg. Aim for the release of the beanbag in coordination with the bowling action. This same release timing must be used when playing games such as hopscotch.

Beanbag crisscross walking

Place twelve differently colored beanbags in matched pairs (two red, two yellow, two green, etc.), on the right and left side. The child steps on the first beanbag on the right with his left foot, then crosses over to the beanbag on the left with his right foot and so on down the line of beanbags.

Other activities

With the beanbag on the floor, ask the child to jump and hop over the beanbag, forward, backward, stand on it, walk toe/heel, creep, and hop around it.

- Don't forget to name the colors.
- In the throwing game, release of the beanbag requires temporal awareness (rate, timing, and sequence).
- Sensory perceptual motor activities reinforce integration, without which movement skills cannot advance.

BALLS

- Balls are great for hand/eye coordination and language skills. Language and movement activities go together.
- Start with medium balls and move to smaller balls.

Use medium-sized balls in soft foam or blow-up balls. Smaller balls require faster tracking and timing and are often difficult to catch. Aim for your child to be successful. Practice forges new pathways in the brain.

Overarm throw

Ask your child to grip a tennis ball–sized foam ball firmly in his hand, touch his ear with the ball, step forward with the foot opposite to his throwing hand, and throw the ball to you, with a bent to full arm.

Finger manipulation of a ball

Child holds a ball with the fingers and thumb of both hands, then with four fingers only, and rotates the ball forward and backward. Try this with three fingers, then two, then do the same with the ball on the floor, around both legs, changing hands at the back, then a figure eight in and out around each leg.

HOOPS

- By this age your child's brain will be twice as active as your adult one.
- These activities require a series of hoop motion and control skills.

Hoop-rolling

Can your child keep rolling the hoop around? Get him to hold the hoop upright and jump forward and backward over the hoop edge. Then he lets the hoop drop to the floor, hops into it, and sits down.

This is a five-sequence challenge. Leave off the last challenge if it's beyond him!

Spin and throw

Try to jump into the hoop and out again before the spinning hoop lands flat.

Throw the hoop in the air, stand still, and catch it before it lands.

Hoops enhance sensory functioning through motor experiences designed to provide specific types of visual, tactile, kinesthetic, and auditory stimulation. Hoops also help to develop self-confidence and self-awareness. The timing of when to grasp and let go of the hoop as you judge its distance and speed is sometimes difficult, and may take several practices to get right. Repetition is nature's way to help the brain tackle these skills.

ROPES AND CORDS

- Ropes now replace ribbons.
- What your child sees and feels must match so that his brain can make sense of it.

Rope-turning

With one hand, get your child to turn the cord or rope in a circle, beside, above, and in front of him. Then repeat using his other hand. He must get the rhythm for timing.

Repetitive jumping develops rate, rhythm, and timing, which we call temporal awareness. Cord and rope activities help increase coordination and flexibility of both the mind and the body, while continuing development of the basic skills. From conception, the foundations are being laid for the more complex task of skipping with a rope, which requires coordination of leg, hand, eye, body, and arm muscles.

Hopping and jumping the rope

Tell your child to hold one end of the cord or rope just in front of his feet with both hands. He then jumps over and back without moving the rope. Next, ask him to try hopping over the rope with his right foot, then his left foot, and back. Now ask him to hold both ends of the rope; let it swing back and forth as he jumps over it, forward and backward.

VISION

- This age group has dramatically improved eye-movement skills due to integration.
- Visual exercises are easier when done with the child lying down, as the forces of gravity are less. So, for full value, eye exercises must be done in the upright position.
- The activities below require the child to watch a hanging ball without moving his head.
- Continue previous visual tracking exercises.

Visual accommodation

Hold the object to be tracked as the child watches it slowly coming to about 2 inches from his nose, then out again. Stop if the object becomes "double." Then he holds the object and brings it slowly to within 2 inches of his eyes.

Creeping with accent on eye/hand vision

Child creeps in cross-pattern, turning his head, alternating from side to side, as he directs his eyes at his forward hand.

Eye-training exercises must not last more than one minute. Using a gross motor movement along with a hand/eye movement while hitting a swinging ball is a challenge. Think of all the skills being developed in the brain, especially his near-point vision (so important to reading). Eyes and body parts must also work together for balance.

Kicking a hanging ball

Lower ball to the level of your child's feet, then ask him to kick it with alternate feet, naming each foot "right" and "left." The opposite arm to the foot will swing forward for balance (cross-pattern).

A professional eyesight check is advisable before school age.

VISUALIZATION

This is the age of fantasy, when children love to play "make believe" about things they have seen. Experiences are visualized both internally (through movement) and externally. Early word and sentence recognition and even adult reading and spelling are primarily achieved through visualization.

Dress up and pretend

These are favorites for this age group. Children get ideas from books you read to them, and also from visits to the shops, the zoo, the beach, and other places. Provide boxes for posting letters, cubby house play, and pretend cooking.

Drawing and painting

With increased awareness of their bodies, children tend to draw people mainly as bodies.

Drawings may be unclear, but adults can generally figure what they are!

Matching pictures and words

Be sure to take photos and pamphlets from the places your child visits. Make a scrap-book, with a picture on one page and a word or two about the picture on the opposite page. Play matching word-to-picture or word-to-word games. Ask questions. Can your child remember/visualize your visit?

Many parents are already "flashing" word and individual picture cards four times daily (words should be on white 8-inch-square cards to help them stand out). Change the card daily and play matching games with the cards that have been "flashed." However the pictures or cards are flashed, visualization will occur. Food store signs are also visualized at a very young age by constantly driving past them!

STAGE H: 4½–5½ YEARS

The exercises and activities for children in this age group aim to ensure that all the prerequisite skills for successful learning have been attained before entry to school.

These include motor skills; the sensory, perceptual, and sequential skills, and fine motor abilities. It is also important to confirm that all the basic primary reflexes have been overcome and the postural ones are present, as the existence of primitive reflexes can cause problems in the attainment of literacy and general learning.

Basic school readiness depends on muscles working together. Just standing motionless depends on the proper tension and extension of two hundred opposing muscles. Skipping-rope activities require the coordination of leg, hand, eye, body, and arm muscles—the precision of muscle control is remarkable.

All of this has been happening in a predictable sequential development from conception. It has taken years, which is why physical therapy for children with developmental difficulties or school underachievement must be undertaken daily, as early as possible. The best way is preventative care, which is the reason for the existence of such centers as Toddler Kindy Gymba-ROO for preventative parental care (also known internationally as KindyROO and AussieROO).

MASSAGE: CROCODILE & COMMANDO POSITIONS

- Massage time is not tickle time—it should be relaxing.
- The crocodile/commando change and forward movement is the most effective activity for overcoming any minor difficulties in neurological development affecting learning and behavior.

Massage in commando position

Massage to different rhymes while your child is lying on her front in the cross-pattern commando position.

Rolling from one side to the other

a. Ask the child to put her hands above her head, turn her head to the right, and roll on to her back.

b. To do a half-roll, she bends up the left knee, places her left arm across her body to the shoulder and, pushing with her left foot, rolls on to her side. The left arm then pushes backward from the floor, the left leg straightens, and the right leg bends up to push, rolling her on to her back. Repeat five times *slowly*.

Crocodile and commando changes

To relax your child, sing or talk quietly while you massage, then start the *very slow* cross-pattern change. Alter the movement of arms and legs so that she does the one-sided crocodile change/crawl forward, then the cross-pattern commando change/crawl.

Commando forward movement is easier on a slippery surface. Ask your child to commando crawl up the vinyl, then have fun whizzing her back!

SQUIRMING, CRAWLING, AND CREEPING

- Provide your child with animal storybooks.
- For these exercises, choose animals that squirm or crawl along the ground or creep on all fours for her to imitate.

Worm squirm

A slippery surface such as vinyl matting helps when your child is a squirmy worm!

Ask her to move one body side and then the other like a worm. Make the movements slow to dodge the traffic! Then ask her to roll over and over, keeping an eye on the edge of the vinyl.

Imitating animals is great sensory stimulation, as these actions are multi-sensory in nature. Bounding is two arms forward together, then two legs together, thus identifying and stimulating the bottom half and then the top half of the body.

Rabbit

Child squats and bounds like a rabbit bounding for its burrow. First, hands "bound" forward, then up jump the feet. This is called bounding on all fours.

TUMBLING, ROCKING, SWINGING

- The vestibular system effect on muscle tone and motor output is well known.
- Muscle tone is also vital to reflex inhibition and neurological development.
- Children slow to develop good vestibular functioning frequently have difficulty maintaining posture and balance.
- Children love activities that stimulate their vestibular functions. Give these "play" activities lots of encouragement.

Forward-tumbling, swinging, spinning

On a mat, try forward-tumbling to standing. Be sure your child's head is tucked close to her chest. Don't allow tumbling over on her head, as she can hurt her neck. Try a running tumble to standing. Swing or spin on a trapeze, rope, swing—or anything that swings!

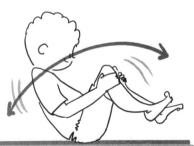

Rocking

From a crouched position, the child then rolls backward by crossing the ankles and clasping the bent legs to the chest with her arms. Then ask her to rock back and forth.

Rocking is very stimulating to a child's neurological development. Rocking backward and forward is not easy, and your child may need a slight push on the back of her head for the rock forward. Vestibular input is necessary for muscle and balance development, eye-tracking ability, and motor planning.

BALANCE

A balance beam is a timber beam 5 feet long, 3½ inches thick, and 1¾ inches wide. It can be used on the floor or raised at each end on one or two wide books.

Heel/toe walk

Ask your child to heel/toe walk on the floor, then on the balance beam, forward, then backward. Arms can be out sideways for balance, looking up at an object at eye level.

Support her from behind, lightly tapping under her elbow. Start with the beam on the floor, then raise it. Repeat five times.

Children play with balance as they walk along the pavement edges, fences, etc. When they move, using balance and posture, and act, explore, manipulate, observe, describe, and make use of the objects in their world, the brain pathways are activated.

Cross-pattern walk

Child balances on a square balance board, tips to the right, and points to an object on the floor to her right with her left hand, then tips to her left side pointing with her right hand to an object on the floor to her left. Repeat five times.

MINI-TRAMPOLINE

- If these activities are new to your child, start with the previous mini-trampoline activities (page 128).
- Sometimes it is easier for the child to try these activities on the floor before attempting them on the mini-trampoline.
- Check the safety rules on page 108.

Sequential commands and activities are now increased. Mini-trampolines are excellent for balance, laterality, body and space awareness, internal nerve endings in the muscles and ligaments, movement control, and hand/eye coordination while moving.

Sequential auditory commands

1. Jump three times, stop. Jump four times, stop.
2. Jump three times, stop. Repeat six times, stop.

These commands can decrease or increase in difficulty. The child must be successful.

Rebounder commands are great for left/right arm and leg actions, cross-pattern jogging and marching, or quarter- and half-turns. Remember, right arm up and over to turn right; then as your child jumps around, left arm up and over to turn left. Try multiple instructions, right arm up, left leg forward. Make up sequences to her ability.

"jump six times—STOP!"

"jump three times—STOP!"

"left leg forward

"right arm up . . ."

"right arm forward

"left arm up . . ."

Moving and thinking

Child catches a ball while jumping, then throws it back underhand. Her feet should stay together when jumping. Include thinking games, songs, simple number games, or other memory games while doing this exercise.

CROSS-PATTERN ACTIONS

Cross-pattern movements stimulate both sides of the brain to work together and are essential for children to achieve well both academically and socially. It is the ultimate normal pattern of adult balanced movements, and enables the development of further skills.

Cross-pattern crawl/commando crawl

Your child should do at least five minutes of cross-pattern commando crawl each day, plus two of the following cross-pattern activities for three minutes each day:

- Cross-pattern throwing.
- Cross-pattern knee-tapping while marching to music.
- Cross-pattern walking (to the shops, etc.), arms swinging.
- Cross-pattern touching toes.
- Cross-pattern walking and pointing to the right toe with the left finger, then the other side.
- Cross-pattern hurdling.
- Cross-pattern running in slow motion.

Skipping

Skipping requires hopping alternately in rhythm, and coordination of the two sides of the brain (each side of the brain runs the opposite side of the body). Children love to skip—they skip everywhere! All young children should skip in a balanced way, with their arms moving well in a cross-pattern manner.

Cross-pattern movements activate development of the nerve pathways between the two hemispheres of the brain to get the two sides of the body working together in a more balanced and coordinated way for efficient movement. They require constant practice from 2½ years to adulthood.

AEROBIC DANCE

- Aerobic activities increase the supply of oxygen from the heart to the body.
- Exercises and dance go together and are easy at this age. There are many aerobic dance and exercise CDs available; look for one that is not too fast for a child's motor planning ability.
- Skipping is an excellent aerobic or dancing activity—all children going into school should be skipping. If boys do not learn to skip before school, they often miss out on this excellent vestibular activity.

Dancing

Choose a dance or aerobic activity that lasts about three minutes. It should be challenging. Give your child a chance to learn the routine before changing to another dance regime. Change the routine after two weeks.

There are many children's shows on TV that contain dances, movements and songs. Just watching TV is not developmentally stimulating. Encourage your child to join in with TV movement shows suitable for her age.

All dance and exercise regimes help listening skills, motor planning and language, with fast and slow tempos and lots of action words, such as sweeping, flying high and low, etc. This involves visualization. Deep breathing should follow exercises.

REST PERIOD WITH MOZART

The music of Mozart, Haydn, and Vivaldi has specific structures that, when electronically enhanced, provide maximum micromassage of the inner ear. These special recordings are referred to as *sound therapy*. Sound therapy recordings are used for many purposes connected to hearing, including for children with auditory processing difficulties. Many are adapted specifically for young children and babies.

There are many other classical music CDs from the Baroque period that are recommended for relaxation and to improve listening skills and learning. Scientific study has shown that this music provides the kind of nourishment that will actively support optimum brain development in a child's early years from infancy. Some are for concentration, some soothing and relaxing, while others stimulate.

Relaxation

Deep breathing while counting in and out. Encourage your child to listen to the different sounds around her. Discuss which are loud and which are soft.

Auditory discrimination listening games

Try this while your child is resting. Can she identify the jangling of keys, jingling of money, moving a chair, tapping a pencil, or crumpling paper? Ask her to cover or close her eyes and point in the direction of a bell you are ringing. With her lying in the commando position, call out the names of fruits, vegetables, furniture, etc. at random, and ask her to change position when she hears the name of a fruit.

HOMEMADE BAND

Rhythm sticks, maracas, homemade bangers, scrapers, rattles, pluckers, or anything else that makes a noise provide lots of fun—and learning, too!

Shakers, Rattles, Bangers, Scrapers

Shakers and rattles from earlier years and upturned ice cream containers make great drums—use wooden spoons for the bangers. Get your child to hear the beat by clapping before using the instruments. Make scrapers with plastic piping bent into a circle. Plug the ends and

join together with a piece of wood, or use as straight pieces and scrape with a stick. Corrugated plumbing pipe makes a great noise if a stick is rubbed up and down it! All kinds of things can be used to make a rhythm band. Ask your child to pretend (visualize) being the bandleader, twirling and flipping the rhythm stick from hand to hand. This may take a little practice.

Rhythm perception is a vital part of coordination, the basis of all movement.
This is an essential prerequisite for development and school readiness.
It is called temporal awareness: rate, rhythm, and timing.
This can be a good family time together.

RHYTHM STICKS

Quick motor planning, color recognition, sequencing of movement, and finger flexibility are functions of our brains, which improve with use!

> If a child is well integrated, there should be no motor overflow to the stationary limb. However, everyone develops at a different rate. These sticks offer a wide variety of movement skills, from the easy to the more challenging skills of rhythm, coordination, dexterity, and balance.

Tapping opposite body parts

Standing up, get your child to hold a stick of the same color in each hand. Tap sticks horizontally four times, tap opposite toes four times, then tap sticks upright end to end four times. Tap colored ends again four times, then tap the right side followed by the left. Repeat five times. Body parts to be tapped can be changed.

Do this exercise quickly!

Finger crawling

Child holds a rhythm stick horizontally in each hand. Using fingers only, turn the sticks in both hands in a circular manner, then one hand at a time, making sure the stationary hand is not moving. Then holding one stick upright in each hand, make each hand crawl up its own stick separately. Keep that non-crawling hand still!

BEANBAGS

Beanbags are used as a teaching tool for the development of many skills, particularly hand/eye coordination, balance, and, at this age, motor planning laterality, body image, and visual tracking skills.

These activities are not easy. If unsuccessful, try dropping the beanbag hand to hand, across the body from left to right hand, then right to left, and gradually increase the distance.

Beanbag drop, catch, and throw

Standing up, the child drops the beanbag from above her head and catches it between her right and left hands. How high apart can she do this? Then throw up the beanbag and catch, first with both hands, then individual hands, right then left.

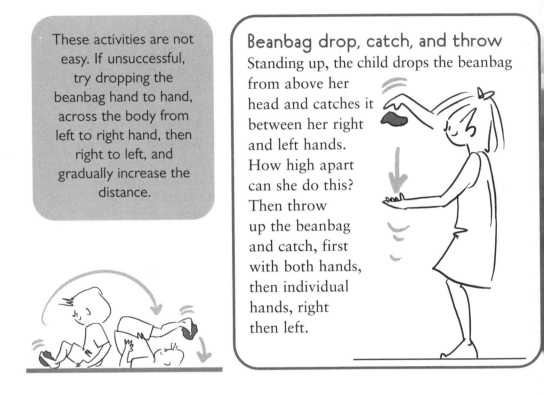

Beanbag rock

Child holds the beanbag tightly between her feet and lifts up her legs, rocking backward, touching the beanbag to the floor behind her head, then rocks back to sitting without dropping the beanbag. She rocks back again, holding the beanbag in her feet, leaving it on the floor behind her head. Back in a sitting position again, she picks up the beanbag with her feet and rocks back to sitting.

BALLS

Dribbling a ball is similar to bouncing it. The ball is not caught, but pushed back down to the ground with the fingertips. Use a medium-sized ball.

Throwing and stopping a ball require exact timing, space awareness, and coordinated movements among the fingers, arms, and eyes. Dribbling, throwing, and stopping a ball are just a few activities with balls. Balls are great for sensory motor stimulation. Ensure that your child has access to them—and in all sizes!

Throwing, bouncing, catching, rolling

Ask your child to bounce the ball high to you. How many times can she bounce and catch the ball? Try dribbling the ball around the room, then bouncing it between the rungs of a ladder lying on its side, or rolling it around your legs in a figure eight.

Overarm cross-pattern throw

Your child grips a foam ball (the size of a tennis ball), touches it to her ear on the same side as her throwing hand, steps forward with the foot on the opposite side, and throws the ball full arm to you. Remind her to judge the strength of her throw to the distance away from you.

HOOPS

Hoops are used mainly in physical education situations. More children should have them at home, though, as they provide stimulating movement activities.

Hoop skipping

Show your child how to skip with a hoop. She holds the hoop upright in front of her feet and jumps over the bottom of it, brings it around over her head and back to the floor. She then jumps over it again.

Hoop hopscotch

See the illustration for the hopscotch hoop pattern.

Child throws a stone into the first hoop, jumps or hops in to pick it up, and hops out.

Repeat this with each hoop each turn, hopping out through the hoops to the start position and throwing the stone into the next hoop. At two hoops, the child jumps into one hoop, then the other. She is out if the throw into the next hoop misses, or if she overbalances while hopping.

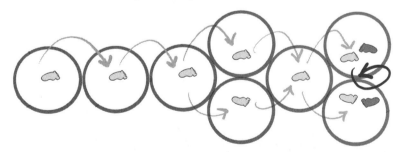

Hoops were once part of everyone's childhood—rolling them along, jumping, and playing with them. Such games as hopscotch help children develop more brain interconnections through balancing, jumping, motor planning, rhythm, sequencing, muscle tone, and sensory stimulation. Lining up and taking turns are also important concepts to learn.

ROPES AND CORDS

These activities are developmental fun, involving jumping, hopping, balancing, and eye/foot stimulation.

- Tug-of-war with a rope is fun and helps the muscles in the arms develop muscle tone.
- Ropes, when used for any activity, require supervision for safety. Where possible use wool cords. A rope ladder is a challenge to climb to get up to that playhouse, though!
- All these activities stimulate children's brains as they move through space in varying ways.

Jumping the rope
The child holds the rope with one end in each hand behind her heels, turns the rope forward over her head, then drags it back toward her feet. She jumps over the rope just before it reaches her toes. This sequence of actions is repeated, gradually turning the rope faster!

Jumping a wiggly cord
Wiggle the rope back and forth on the floor, and ask the child to jump over the rope snake without touching it. Alternatively, swing the rope low to the ground in a circle of about 8 feet, and ask her to jump over it as it swings around. It might help to attach a ball to the end of the rope.

VISION

Hand/eye coordination needs lots of repetition and practice for the pathways in the brain to be firmly established. These activities are very helpful at this age.

Rolling with open vision

The child lies in a prone position on the floor with hands over her head and body straight—like a pencil. Her eyes are level with a line like the carpet edge. As she rolls over, she must watch the line and keep her body straight. You could also use a ball as a target to watch while rolling over.

Using gross motor movements with simultaneous hand/eye movements is a challenge. For a child to time the movement of the ball in order to hit it with her foot at the same time as she performs a hand-action requires muscle control and motor planning. Think of all the skills being developed in the brain.

Swinging ball

Hang a ball at eye level and ask your child to hit it with alternate hands, while raising the knee on the same side, and then the knee on the other side. Lower the ball and hit it with alternate knees, while swinging the arm forward on the same side, then the opposite side. Lower the ball and kick it with alternate feet, with the arm pointing to the foot on the same side. Do this ten times each side.

Remember: Preschool vision checks are advisable.

VISUALIZATION

- Visualization is developed through motor sensory experiences.
- Games involving counting and basic word or picture recognition, and even motor movements such as riding a bicycle, rely on internal visualization.

Visualize

Ask your child to be an animal—can you guess which one? Play hidey!

Short stories

Read your child her favorite short stories and run your finger under each word.

Children learn through exposure and repetition.

There are excellent DVD stories with underlined prose for the child to follow and learn through visual repetition.

Play matching games

Play matching word cards with the pictures in your child's scrapbook showing the places they have been to and the things she has visualized as a result of her experiences. Be sure to add new pictures and words. Don't ask "What word is this?" Just show the card and say what it reads. This game must be fun. Do not show the picture and the word on the same card!

If successful, start the words from Ladybird Books 1 and 2—there are word lists at the end of each book. Do one page at a time and do *not* give your child the book until all words have been flashed, four times daily (one second each). Flash seven words on plain cardboard 9 inches square. Flash a new word each day and remove an old one. Play games with the words and add the odd card with two or three previously flashed words.

BIBLIOGRAPHY

Aoki, C., and P. Steketvitz, "Plasticity in Brain Development," *Scientific American* 259(6), 56-64, 1988.

Arnheim, D. D., and W. A. Sinclair, *The Clumsy Child* (second edition), St. Louis, C. V. Mosby, 1979.

Ayres, A. J., *Sensory Integration and Learning Disorders*, Los Angeles, Western Psychological Services, 1974.

Bakker, R. D. J., *Neuropsychological Treatment for Dyslexia*, Oxford, Oxford University Press, 1990.

Bérard, G., *Hearing Equals Behavior*, Connecticut, Keats Publishing, 1993.

Berthoz, Alain, *The Brain's Sense of Movement*, Boston, Harvard University Press, 2000.

Blythe, S. A. Goddard, *The Well Balanced Child*, Hawthorne Press, 2004.

Cade, R., *Research on Autism and Schizophrenia*, Florida, University of Florida, 1998–99.

Campbell, D., *The Mozart Effect*, New York, Avon Books, 1997.

Chandler, E. H., *The Shape of Intelligence*, London, Allen & Unwin, 1970.

Delacato, C. H., *The Diagnosis of Speech and Reading Problems*. Springfield, Charles C. Thomas, 1970.
—*The Ultimate Stranger, Your Autistic Child*, New York, Doubleday, 1974.

Dengate, S., *Fed Up*, Sydney, Random House, 1998.

Doidge, Norman, *The Brain that Changes Itself*, Melbourne, Scribe Publications, 2007.

Domain, R., "The Philosophical Core," in *The Listening Program*, Philadelphia, Advanced Brain Technologies, 1999.

Doman, G., D. Doman, and B. Hagy, *How to Teach your Child to be Physically Superb*, Philadelphia, The Better Baby Press, 1988.

Epstein, H. T., "Stages in Human Brain Development," *Developmental Brain Research* 30, 114–19, 1986.

Ganong, W. F., *Review of Medical Physiology*, Englewood Cliffs, Prentice Hall, 1987.

Gesell, A., *Infant Development*, Connecticut, Greenwood Press, 1952.

Getman, G., *How to Develop Your Child's Intelligence*, Los Angeles, Optometric Extension Program Foundation, 1995.

Glascoe, F. P., "The value of parents' concerns to detect and address developmental and behavioral problems," *Journal of Pediatrics and Child Health* 35 (1), 1–8, 1999.

Goddard, S. A., *A Teacher's Window into a Child's Mind*, Eugene, Fern Ridge Press, 1996.

Healy, J. M., *Endangered Minds*, Touchstone, Simon & Schuster, 1990.

Held, R., "Plasticity in Sensory Motor Systems," Readings from *Scientific American*, 1965.

Holt, T. K. S., *Child Development*, Oxford, Butterworth and Heinemann, 1993.

Ibuka, M., *Kindergarten is Too Late*, London, Sphere Books, 1977.

Kandell, E. R., J. H. Schwartz, and T. M. Jessell, *Principles of Neural Science* (third edition), Connecticut, Appleton & Lange, 1991.

Klosovskii, P. N., *The Development of the Brain and its Disturbance by Harmful Factors*, Oxford, Pergamon Press, 1963.

Krebs, C., *A Revolutionary Way of Thinking*, Melbourne, Hill of Content Publishing, 1988.

Levine, S., "Stimulation in Infancy," *Scientific American* 7, 55-61, 1960.

Le Winn, E. B., *Neurological Organization*, Springfield, Charles C. Thomas, 1965.

Maduale, P., *When Listening Comes Alive*, Canada, Moulin Publishing, 1994.

McCain, M. N., J. F. Mustard, and S. Shanker, *Early Years Study 2: Putting Science into Action*, Toronto, Council for Early Childhood Development, 2007.

Morris, D., *Baby*, London, Hamlyn, 2008.

Nash, M., "Fertile Minds," *Time Magazine*, 149 (5), 36–46, 1997.

Piaget, J., *The Origins of Intelligence*, International Universities Press, 1969.

Pretchl, H., "General movement assessment as a method of developmental neurology: New paradigms and their consequences," *Developmental Medicine & Child Neurology* 43 (12), 836–842, 2001.

Sassé, M. K. K., *If Only We'd Known* (fifth edition), Melbourne, Toddler Kindy GymbaROO, 1990.

—*Tomorrow's Children*, Melbourne, Toddler Kindy GymbaROO, 2002.

Sheridan, M. D., *From Birth to Five Years*, Melbourne, ACER, 1973. (Revised and updated by M. Frost and A. Sharma, 1997.)

Shore, R., *Rethinking the Brain*, New York, Families and Work Institute, 1997.

White, B., *Raising a Happy Unspoiled Child*, Simon & Schuster, New York, 1994.

Williams, J., "Helping parents help their children: an innovative Australian program." *American Academy of Pediatrics Behavioral and Developmental Newsletter* 16 (1), 18–19, 2007.

INDEX

Angels in the sand 90, 125
animals 66, 74, 96, 103, 111, 123, 141
autism 156
awareness: body and space 16, 19, 25, 57,
    60, 61, 78, 82, 89, 90, 95, 99, 123, 125;
    body 17, 21, 27, 55, 68, 78, 87, 89,
    90–98, 104, 107, 109, 112–116, 125,
    129, 138, 144, 148, 151; color 48, 79,
    85, 101; space/spatial 10, 35, 47, 56, 67;
    temporal 11, 57, 79, 82, 83, 104, 133,
    136; language 87; parental 81; self-
    awareness 125; fingers 107

balance 11, 16, 20, 22, 25, 29, 31, 36,
    37, 40, 44–47, 51, 52, 54, 57, 60, 67,
    72, 76, 77, 78, 85, 88, 89, 94, 95, 108,
    112, 113, 117, 120, 121, 126, 128,
    129, 137, 141, 142, 144, 145, 150,
    151, 152, 156
balls 18, 42, 45, 53, 58, 59, 60, 61, 65, 71,
    77, 78, 83, 91, 99, 102, 112, 118, 121,
    134, 137, 151, 153, 154
bilateral 10, 50, 54, 67
bobbing 29, 36, 38, 48, 49, 54, 57, 64, 67,
    69, 80, 92, 111, 119
brain development 13, 17, 18, 29, 33, 35,
    43, 44, 47, 75, 76, 90, 94, 97, 100, 122,
    143, 147, 154
breast feeding 15, 20

climbing 10, 36, 48, 64
commando 14, 34, 43, 105, 114, 124, 140,
    145, 147
creeping 19, 39, 42, 43, 44, 46, 47, 48, 49,
    54, 56, 85, 106, 114, 121, 137, 141
cruising 39, 46, 49, 54

dancing 16, 25, 51, 64, 80, 95, 115

environment 11–14, 17, 24, 40, 53, 58, 81,
    109, 123

fingers 18, 19, 40, 41, 60, 69, 73, 74, 106,
    107, 114, 116, 118, 134, 149, 151
food intolerance 14
foundations 13, 136
frequency, intensity, and duration 13, 35,
    105, 107

homemade 60, 63, 79, 148
homolateral 89
hoops 84, 100, 119, 135, 152
hopping 10, 109, 126, 130, 136, 145, 152,
    153
hypersensitive 96

inner ear 11, 13, 16, 17, 22, 25, 29, 32, 44,
    60, 65, 92, 110, 147

learning 14, 24, 44, 48, 49, 50, 52, 56, 60,
    62, 86, 87, 105, 106, 109, 115, 122, 123,
    124, 139, 140, 147, 148, 156

massage 13–19, 26, 28, 34, 36, 40, 41, 55,
    68, 69, 89, 105, 124, 140, 147
midline 55, 83, 97, 107, 109, 117, 121,
    127, 128, 129
muscle tone 10, 11, 16, 17, 18, 20, 21,
    23–28, 35–38, 42-8, 50–52, 55, 57, 59,
    61, 65, 67, 69, 72, 73, 78, 81, 83, 90, 91,
    94, 97, 101, 104–106, 126, 127, 136,
    139, 142, 144, 153

neurological 71, 123, 126, 140, 142

parachute reflex 11, 35, 58, 61, 65
perception 11, 33, 86, 88, 104, 148
perceptual 11, 65, 81, 86, 123, 133, 139
planning 49, 56, 64, 66, 80, 82, 83, 87, 88,
    89, 95, 100, 115, 119, 142, 146, 149,
    150, 152, 154
postural reflexes 11, 46, 61, 94, 149
posture 22, 29, 78, 88, 112, 129, 142, 143

primitive reflexes 10, 11, 15, 17, 21, 22, 27, 30, 35, 37, 46, 49, 52, 62, 75, 78, 89, 95, 105, 106, 139

rhythm 11, 16, 19, 25, 26, 31, 35, 41, 50, 51, 52, 55, 62, 63, 64, 69, 70, 74, 75, 79, 80, 82, 91, 95, 96, 97, 106, 114, 115, 116, 124, 127, 130, 131, 132, 136, 144, 145, 148, 149, 152
rolling 6, 7, 18, 23, 27, 30, 31, 37, 40, 45, 47, 52, 61, 62, 78, 83, 84, 86, 91, 92, 124, 131, 132, 135, 140, 145, 148, 149, 151, 152, 154

sensations 22, 27, 41, 68, 124, 135
sensory 11, 14, 29, 30, 31, 32, 36, 38, 39, 40, 43, 44, 47, 51, 53, 54, 76, 80, 81, 88, 89, 90, 95, 97, 104, 105, 106, 114, 116, 118, 123, 133, 135, 139, 141, 151, 152, 155, 156
sensory integration 11, 90, 97, 104, 156
sight 32, 53, 103, 125, 137
sitting 30, 34, 35, 38, 42, 44, 46, 52, 59, 71, 75, 78, 83, 84, 91, 94, 96, 98, 110, 112, 119, 127, 129, 131, 150
space 10, 11, 16, 22, 25, 30, 37, 38, 47, 56, 57, 60, 61, 65, 67, 72, 78, 88, 90, 94, 95, 99, 104 115, 117, 123, 126, 127, 130, 144, 151, 153
speech 16, 26, 30, 31, 38, 54, 61, 66, 70, 74, 81, 115, 131, 158
spinning 25, 30, 51, 52, 60, 65, 75, 76, 80, 83, 93, 95, 110, 116, 127, 135, 142
stairs 44, 64, 77

tactile 78, 135
tummy 20–25, 31, 32, 34, 35, 37, 42–47, 54

vestibular 11, 13, 16, 22, 29, 30, 38, 46, 51, 52 60, 61, 62, 75, 76, 78, 79, 80, 91, 92, 93, 94, 108, 110, 126, 127, 128, 142, 146
vision 11, 29, 32, 33, 42, 51, 60, 61, 64, 65, 86 101, 102, 104, 109, 116–118, 121, 127, 136, 137, 154, 155
visualization 11, 52, 62, 66, 79, 87, 91, 96, 103 115, 117, 122, 125, 130, 138, 146, 155

walking 10, 25, 27, 36, 39, 43, 44–46, 49, 54, 56, 58, 64, 72, 73–77, 78, 80, 84, 85, 86, 94, 95, 98, 107, 111, 114, 120, 131, 133, 143, 14